I0092577

INITIATION AND PASTORAL PSYCHOLOGY:

TOWARD AFRICAN PERSONALITY THEORY

PROF JOHN GATUNGU GITHIGA

Initiation and Pastoral Psychology
Copyright © 2022 by Prof John Gatungu Githiga

All rights reserved. No part of this publication
may be reproduced, distributed, or transmitted
in any form or by any means, including
photocopying, recording, or other electronic
or mechanical methods, without the prior
written permission of the author, except
in the case of brief quotations embodied
in critical reviews and certain other non-
commercial uses permitted by copyright law.

ISBN
978-1-956161-92-2 (Hardcover)
978-1-956161-91-5 (Paperback)
978-1-956161-90-8 (eBook)

OTHER BOOKS BY THE AUTHOR

The Spirit in the Black Soul

CHRIST AND ROOTS:
Jesus as Revealed in the Bible and the African Traditional Religions

THE HOLY SPIRIT:
The Greatest Promise and the Greatest Gift of All

INITIATION AND PASTORAL PSYCHOLOGY:
Toward African Personality Theory

MINISTRY TO ALL NATIONS:
Practical Theology of Mission and Church Planting

70 SERMONS:
Liturgical Preaching

GOSPEL TO ALL NATIONS:
Preaching from the Lectionary

THE SECRETS OF SUCCESS IN MARRIAGE

25 SECRETS OF SUCCESS IN MARRIAGE

30 SECRETS OF SUCCESS IN MARRIAGE:
A Book for Premarital and Marriage Counseling

SYSTEMATIC THEOLOGY:
An Introduction to the African Theological Voice

FROM VICTORY TO VICTORY

FRUITFUL FAMILY:
Family Therapy Based on Christian Principles

DAILY DEVOTION FOR THE NATIONS

THE HOLY TRINITY AND US:
Viewing the Holy Trinity from Practical Theology Perspective

TABLE OF CONTENTS

Part One

Chapter One

Chapter Two

    A. Definition

    B. Origin of the Gikuyu

    C. The Origin of Irua

    D. The Initiates

    E. Preparation for Irua

    F. The Operation

    G. Seclusion

        1. Killing of the Circumcision Ram

        2. Submissiveness

        3. Sex Education

        4. There was Ceremonial Sexual Intercourse

Chapter Three

Part Two

Chapter Four

Chapter Eight

C. Psychology and Division of Labor

    1. Your Preferences

    2. Naming

    3.Sixteen Personality Types

D. Division of Labor and Counseling

Chapter Nine

A. What is Mararanja?

B. Mararanja and the International Community

Chapter Ten

A. The Structure and Initiation

B. The Structure and Religion

C. The Antistructure and Structure

Chapter Eleven

A. What is Lostness

B. Communal Lostness

C. The Positivity and Negativity of Lostness

D. The Causes and Treatment of Lostness

Chapter Twelve

A. The Particularity and Universality of Pain

B. Pain and Religion

C. Pain and Personality Growth

ABOUT THE AUTHOR

Dr. Githiga is the archbishop of All Nations Anglican Church;, dean and professor of pastoral theology at All Nations Seminary; former chaplain and adjunct faculty at West Texas A&M University and Grambling State University; instructor at Pensacola Junior College; head of the Department of Pastoral Theology at St. Paul's United Theological College, Limuru, Kenya; and the first president of the African Association for Pastoral Study and Counseling. He is a graduate from Church Army College, St. Paul's United Theological College, Makerere University, the University of the South, Vanderbilt University, and the International Bible Institute and Seminary. Dr. Githiga has ministered to the people of many nationalities and races and was recorded in the eighth addition of Who is Who among black Americans. He is married to the Rev. Mary Githiga and they have three children.

Acknowledgements

I give a heartfelt acknowledgment to the late Urban T. Holmes, III, the former dean and professor of theology and culture at the School of Theology and to Dr. Richard A. O'Connor, professor of anthropology at the University of the South, for their constructive advice and for trusting me as a novice in their fields.

Special thanks to my wife, Mary; sisters of St. Mary's Convent Sewanee; and my students and colleagues at St. Paul's Theological College, Pensacola Junior College, and Grambling State University and West Texas A&M University, and All Nations Anglican Seminary .

PREFACE

I am intrigued by the secret of success for the 50 percent of marriages in United States that last. One of these marriages is between a Kikuyu male, Francis, and Janie, an African American female. When I visited with them, they had been married for forty-eight years and have had successive children and grand children.

The secret of their success was that Jannie was a student of cultural anthropology. The discipline gave her great respect for the symbols and rituals of her boyfriend's community. One of the lessons that she learned was that dowry was essential to the Gikuyu and for that reason, she advised her father to ask for a dowry. "I cannot sell my daughter!" was the quick response from her father. Jannie told her father, "Dad, you are not going sell your daughter, but you need to tell them that your daughter is worthy two million dollars. Nevertheless, ask them to give you two dollars on which they will write $1,000,000 on each dollar. Ask them to give you cows. However, since it is difficult to transport animals to American, ask them to give animal carvings." This pleased both Jannie's and Francis's parents. After their marriage, Jannie did extensive research on Francis's family tree. Eventually, she was born again into the family. Consequently, they had fruitful marriage.

This book employs anthropological approach to pastoral care and is intended to enhance your interest and respect for other people' culture, as Francis and Jannie exemplified. The first part of the book is a study of the Gikuyu culture. Some students have felt uncomfortable when going through these pages, particularly the introduction, which presents the debate on female circumcision. I need to state that I do not advocate female circumcision, and that this is not an argument for male circumcision. I fully agree with St. Paul: *"Let everyone lead the life which the Lord has assigned to him, and in which God has called him. This is my rule in all the churches. Was any one at the time of his call already circumcised? Let him not seek to remove the marks of his circumcision. Was any one of the time of his call uncircumcised? Let him not seek circumcision. For neither circumcision count for anything nor uncircumcision, but keeping the commandment of God"(I Corinthians 7:17-20)NRSV.* However, the author employs initiation as an observation post through which he views the human life cycle and the deep structure of human beings. As with Jannie and Francis, it is hoped that the insight in this book will equip you with the skills of dealing with different ethnic groups, and thereby extend your ego boundary and enhance your self-identity. It will help you to see the meaning in symbols and rituals, and aid you in exploring the objective psyche—that part of you that is unfathomable and appears in your dreams, particularly when you see yourself in an unknown place with unknown people or animals. It will encourage you to view adolescence from physiological, psychological, sociological, and religious perspectives. Through this book, you will also be able to view your own passages in the light of the passages of Jesus. Ultimately, you will join the author in an attempt to answer a profound question, which is posed by the Psalmist:

> *When I consider your heavens*
> *The work of your fingers,*
> *The moon and the star which you have ordained* **What is man that you are mindful of him? and the son of man that you visit him?** *You have made him a little lower than the angels, And you have crowned him with glory and honor You have made him to have dominion over the works of your hands*
> *You have put all things under his feet*

(Psalm 8:3-6, NKJV)

a

INTRODUCTION

Initiation is one of Africa's unsurpassed contributions to the global village. This important ancient rite has stretched its strong wings and is flying over the Mediterranean Sea to Europe and over the Atlantic Ocean to America. Her wisdom is being employed by western churches for preparing candidates for baptism and confirmation. Her rituals, symbolism, and instructive methodology are used for ushering in adolescents into the world of manhood and womanhood. The most remarkable initiation was organized by Edwina Johnson, an African American at St. George's Episcopal Church. Edwina, who had visited Africa and was impressed by the rites for young men, prepared initiation programs for fourteen black girls. As it is with irua, the purposes for the initiation were to validate the initiates' cultural heritage as they step into the corridor of womanhood, to transmit African cultural heritage and Anglican religious ethos, to support and strengthen them, and to give them a sense of meaning and direction.

The initiators included mature women, teachers, sponsors, a Senegalese woman, and an Akan woman priest. The instruction, which took seven months, comprised of practical homemaking, personal skills, assertive skills, sex education, time management, and African American cultural traditions. As with African initiations, the older women passed their wisdom and ethics to the young ones.

While initiation is being imported by the western countries, it is one of the most debated issues in Kenya. The debate was triggered by unsuccessful operations, which were performed in July, 1982 in West Pokot on a pregnant girl who bled to death. Consequently, the circumciser of this girl was arrested and imprisoned for eighteen months. In August of the same year, nine girls of less than seven years of age were admitted to Wajir Hospital with severe post-circumcision hemorrhage. All the girls recovered after blood transfusions. This incident was followed by the improper circumcision of some boys in Wundanyi Taita Taveta District. Three of the ninety-six boys who were operated on, had their penises amputated and were admitted to Wesu Hospital. According to Dr. M. B. Lugogo's remarks, "Three boys may have a urinary problem, and will not be able to perform sex for the rest of their lives."

These incidents resulted in hostile reactions against the rite. Some medical doctors, who had to deal with the practical problem of giving blood transfusions to the victims, appealed to the government to intervene and change the situation. One of the doctors complained that the instruments used were unsterilized and that they infected the wounds." He advised that the parents who were endangering their children's live "under the pretext of culture and customs should be educated."

In response to this doctor, the director of Medical Services at/for …, Dr. W. K. Koinange, wrote a circular to the Ministry personnel, of which copies were sent to the Catholic Secretariat and the Protestant Churches Medical Association directing that "if anyone felt he could perform the operation he had to receive specific authority from his office."

Furthermore, President Moi condemned female circumcision in a public meeting in Baringo District threatening, "If I hear of a person circumcising girls in this district, he will be on fire," and that those who will be found committing the act or encouraging it will be prosecuted. He contended that people who were circumcising the girls were doing so not because it was healthy, but because they wanted to make a living. The incidents and the statements from the medical doctors and the president provoked a debate of the issue. Numerous articles were published by the local papers on the subject. People of all ethnic groups joined the debate. There were cases for and against circumcision.

In reaction to this position, some writers made an appeal to the government requesting a decree that could make circumcision compulsory to all males in Kenya. One of the correspondents, for example, argued thatuncircumcised male subjects are exposed to health hazardsand for this reason, "authorities concerned should look into this matter with critical eyes and if possible make male circumcision in Kenya compulsory. Nevertheless, the debate was mainly focused on female circumcision. Those who were opposed to the act gave economic, religious, moralistic, modernistic, and biological reasons.

Economical arguments were expressed by the Bukusu and Nandi correspondents. It was contended that in Bukusu land, thousands of cattle are slaughtered and there is no way to recover them after the ceremony. The families travel from one place to another and consequently incur unnecessary expenses. There is also lack of sexual morality, since during circumcision dances there are "free sexual mix-ups."

In Nandi, it was complained that apart from being a risky exercise, the expense involved in the preparation of food, drink, decoration, and many other items exceed Kshs 4,500 (US$562). This excludes some Kshs 2,000, incurred when making the arrangement for the girl to come out of hiding after one month. The correspondent complained that the expenses could pay the school fees for two students in a secondary school.

Those who gave religious arguments hold that female circumcision is neither willed by God nor documented in the Bible. They agrued that Just like the removal of teeth, which is not necessary, circumcision is against God's will. Otherwise, God would have created men without foreskins and women without clitoris. In addition, if we follow the Bible closely, there is no indication that females were or should be circumcised. Those who gave moralistic arguments lamented that during the initiation ceremonies, theft, rape, and sexual immorality are usually on the increase.

The modernists regarded female circumcision as something of the past, which should disappear just as cannibalism has disappeared. A Luo correspondent advised that, Just as the Luo have accepted change and have abandoned the removal of six teeth and are already beginning to decide on whether to circumcise men or not, please accept changes.

Biologically, it was argued that female circumcision causes severe bleeding and that there is a danger of being infected with tetanus from the use of septic tools. In addition, the hardened scar from some operations may complicate the first delivery of a child. Furthermore, the operation may cause urinary retention, bladder injury, damage to the anus, infertility, and chronic pelvic infections. Worse still, the excision of the clitoris may cause frigidity and deprive a woman of sexual enjoyment. "To circumcise women," lamented a moderator of Presbyterian General Assemble, "was the same as castrating them because it deprived them of sexual pleasure and also gave them pain during childbirth."

There was also a contention that the modern method of circumcision is devoid of initiation since it does not include training for adult behavior—it is not an initiation per se. Those who hold this view argued that modern circumcision is without ritual and teaching, which traditionally transmitted the whole gamut of values, norms, and customs to an individual community.

The majority of the people who strongly defended female circumcision were reacting against those who attacked the rite. They expressed their deep sentiment about this form of initiation. A woman who is a shopkeeper, for instance, realizing that I am a priest, confronted me with these words, "You have banned female circumcision, but this very year, we have circumcised more than ever." Another woman who is a circumciser, and a daughter of a circumciser, was reported to have said, "Stop it in the town, but in Manyatta, we shall continue." Some women who have undergone the rite, not only had strong sentiments in favor of circumcision, but they went as far as attempting to circumcise the uncircumcised women. For example, in Wajir District, a woman named Rukia threatened to circumcise a female nurse. Rukia was arrested, taken to court and was fined Kshs 100 (US$10.00).

Those who made a counter-attack refuted the ideas that female circumcision is irreligious, immoral, outdated, and uneconomical. It was argued that circumcision is a religious act in that Abraham and Jesus were circumcised. Better still, they were operated on at home and none of them either had severe bleeding or penis amputation. They were never taken to the hospital. For this reason, people should be circumcised traditionally and at home. Hospital circumcision should be avoided.

Moreover, circumcision is vital since it connects the people concerned with their primordial time. According to Juma wa Khalakanji, during the rite, the Bukusu commemorate the heroic act of Mango, who in ancient days, killed a big snake that used to kill many Bukusu and Mount Elgon Masai. After killing the snake, there was a celebration, whereby, Mango was circumcised at a mature age.

The argument that circumcision is an extravagant exercise was refuted. The Bukusu, for instance, argued that the slaughtering of animals during circumcision ceremony is not a waste, but a kind of offering which the Bukusu society presents to their God, "Were," and in return, the initiates were blessed.

With regard to culture, it was contended that initiation is one of the few remaining vestiges of our culture and to abandon it means abandoning the African culture and become sons and daughters of Europe. Female circumcision should, therefore, continue since it does not only help girls to get husbands, but also enhances their dignity as African women. Moreover, circumcision is regarded as one of the means of instilling morality in the community. During initiation, boys and girls are trained to respect their parents and the aged. The initiates are, in return, respected by those who are younger than them. According to a Kisii correspondent, an initiated Kisii woman "has to respect her father seriously." Accordingly, she is also given more freedom to interact with young men. If, however, a girl decides to remain uncircumcised, she is considered unhealthy, a coward, and un-Kisii.

Interestingly, some circumcised women argued that female circumcision enhances sex morality. This is so because when the clitoris is removed, it enables women to exercise self-control. Consequently, they are able to control the males. This contention was well articulated by Mama Kali. She contended that one of the main reasons behind circumcision was to hold in check their (men) lust. She therefore appealed to other women, support her since one way of holding in check the lust of our men is "to cut it off". She maintained that circumcision in men does not help in curbing their lust.

One of the greatest champions of female circumcision is a Samburu female circumciser named Naimeko. Naimeko defended herself as a professional, claiming that she underwent training for many days and that none of the girls she circumcised had died. She regards the practice as important in that it earns her a living. Besides, circumcision is compulsory for Samburu girls. It is a means of preparation for and a part of marriage ceremonies. "A girl may run away," said Naimeko, "but if she has to marry, we will have to circumcise her before she goes." An uncircumcised girl cannot get a man to marry her. So, for Naimeko, circumcision is an important aspect of Samburu life, for it makes a girl Samburu.

The above arguments indicate that initiation is essential in that it is an African traditional school of belief, which imparts societies' ethics, norms, values, and goals and is one of the vehicles that transmits culture from one generation to another and brings families together for sanctification of life, time, and space.

Surprisingly, the 1982 debate on circumcision unearthed more data about the practice. We learned, for instance, that Western societies are not excluded from the practice of female circumcision. In England, Denmark, and France, European women are being circumcised. According to The Observer, doctors at private London clinics carry out about a dozen female circumcisions each year. The procedure involves the surgical removal of the clitoris. Dr. Sunit Ghatak, who has an office on Harley Street agreed that he carries out about one female circumcision a year. He said, "I do not encourage the operation because there is no medical reason or advantage. But if one comes in because of suffering depression and all that—then we do it." Moreover, while an African female circumciser charges less than Kshs 1, a European doctor charges between $1,360 and $1,700. While Dr. Ghatak saw no medical value in female circumcision, he seemed to imply that there may be some psychological advantages. Hence, they operate if someone comes in because of depression.

Nevertheless, the African circumcision for both male and female differs from the Western one. The Western one is a mere operation. For the African, it is an initiation. The Western circumcision is individualistic, while the African one is communal. Furthermore, the Africans undergo the rite as a fulfillment of the community requirement. The Western circumcision is devoid of rituals; the African one is ritualized. The main purpose of this work, however, is not to compare and contrast the Western circumcision with the African circumcision. Time and energy do not allow me to deal with initiation rites that are performed by various African tribes. The ultimate concern is to study the Gikuyu form of initiation.

Initiation, being a community rite par excellence, is the focal point of African rituals, myths, and symbols. It ritualizes, symbolizes, and externalizes both the inner world and outer world of people. For this reason, we will use this rite as an observation post from which we will view the deep structure and collective unconscious. Since there is a universal psychic unity, it can be asserted that the psychic elements, which are ritualized and externalized by the initiation, are inherent in all human families. Thus, it is believed that this book will increase understanding of the human personality. As such, we will start from the particular and then move to the universal.

It is hoped that this work will be of special interest and give additional skills to psychologists, psychiatrists, counselors, social workers, pastors, and teachers as well as the students of African studies, sociology, social anthropology, theology, and anyone who is eager to understand human personality. The first part of this book will discuss the importance of and give a detailed description of the initiation rite, discuss its' meaningfulness, and put it within the context of the community's life cycle. The second part will view the initiation from physiological, psychological, sociological, and religious perspectives. The third part will conceptualize the initiation motifs with the "passages" of Jesus Christ. The last part will identify the archetypal motifs of human personality, which were ritualized by the Gikuyu initiation. The motifs that will be discussed include communality, individuality, sexuality, division of labor, the antistructure, the structure, lostness, pain, the Tree of God, the Great Mother, and the Great Father.

It should be pointed out that this book will not exhaust all psychic archetypal motifs. Being a pioneer work, the writer regards it as open-minded rather than conclusive.

a

Part One

CHAPTER ONE

The Significance of Irua

Initiation was, and still is, of great importance to the people concerned because it brings them together and is a sanctification of life, time, and space. Traditionally, it was children's greatest anticipation and motivating factor, and was a rite of passage for the parents since it promoted children to mature adulthood Moreover, it is one of the recurring issues in Africa; it influences community's religious expression and externalizes and ritualizes the inner and outer realities of human personality and the community's life cycle.

Professor John Mbiti rightly contends that initiation ceremony was one of the key moments in the rhythm of individual life, which was also a rhythm of the corporate group of which the individual was a part. What happened to a single youth happened corporately to the parents, relatives, neighbors, the living dead, and those yet to be born. It was during and through this rite that the living, the dead, and those yet to be born communicated. All the activities were halted in order that all families could gather.

Thus childhood moved toward and yearned for this great moment. Boys and girls prepared themselves in various ways: they had their ear lobes pierced; their two lower front teeth pulled out, and finally underwent the ritual of second birth (which we be explain later). Children knew that it was only initiation that would make them men and women. Before undergoing the ordeals and instructions of this ancient school, every boy was aware of the fact that he was a child and an almost inactive member of society. Traditionally, a girl could not be a woman without the initiation. Thus, initiation was looked upon as the defining moment in giving a boy or a girl the status of manhood and womanhood. Ngugi wa Thiongo expresses this sentiment in his book *The River Between,* using the characters of Muthoni and Nyambura. The two girls were daughters of Joshua, a preacher, who had agreed with the missionaries that female circumcision should be abolished. For that reason, he could not permit his daughters to be initiated. Nevertheless, initiation was the key issue with the girls. Muthoni, the elder sister, expressed her compelling desire to be circumcised. Nyambura, the younger sister, reminds her that their father would not permit it because he regarded it as antiChristian, antimissionary, wrong, and sinful. But, Muthoni insisted that she shall be circumcised, saying, "I want to become a woman! A real woman, knowing the ways of the hills and the ridges." Muthoni knew very well that unless she underwent the rite, she could remain immature for life and that when she became a big uninitiated girl, she would not be incorporated into the children's or adults' social groups and that she would remain a loner for life.

Worse still, she would miss a schooling, which imparted ethics and customs and introduces an individual to the wisdom and mystery of the tribe. Thus, initiation marked the beginning of acquiring knowledge, which was not accessible to those who were not initiated. It was *sine qua non* for manhood and womanhood since one could not inherit property, participate in war, or marry if he or she had not gone through the rite.

Furthermore, irua exerted enormous influence in the Gikuyu understanding, interpretation, and expression of the Gospel. Most of the Gikuyu Christian folk songs employ irua symbols and language. This point can be illustrated by a song that women sang with me at my farewell party when I was leaving for the United States in 1976. This party was organized by my family at Ichichi, the countryside where I was born. The song went as follows:

Women: Ndukenyenye, Ndukenyenyeke Immovable, immovable remain.

Me: Ndingienyenya, Ndingienyenyeka Immovable, immovable I shall remain.

The verb Ndukenyenyeke means remain immovable, be unshakable, and do not have bodily movement. The word literally explains how the initiate is expected to sit or stand during the initiation rite. All the women who were singing had undergone initiation. I had even seen some of them being circumcised when I was a boy. These women used irua symbols and language to convey Christian challenge to me. Their words were very effective because in the Gikuyu sexual division of labor, during war, the women sounded an alarm, which challenged the men to fight. Throughout my stay in the United States, the two words of the song challenged me. They guided and directed me as the Great Universal Mother. In fact, I was probably unconsciously influenced by this song to do an extensive study on irua.

Thus, the study of irua is of surpassing value to all who are interested in the study of initiations, rites of passages, developmental and analytical psychologies, and faith development. Chapter Two, which gives a detailed description of irua, forms a good basis for comparative study of initiations and is a great resource for Christian thinkers, who view baptism, confirmation, and ordination as initiation. Chapter Three, which views circumcision within the context of a community's life cycle, is of special attraction to the students of analytical psychology and cultural anthropology.

Chapter Four, which gives a clinical reflection of the puberty rite, is of great significance to parents, high school teachers, youth workers, and anyone who is interested in adolescent psychology. It will offer some insights into adolescents' physiological, psychological, social, and religious conflicts, which were ritualized during the mararanja celebration.

Chapter Five will enhance your knowledge of theology of incarnation and offer you a relaxed and attractive safari to your passages and the passages of Jesus Christ, who became all what we are, except sin. You will note how the God-man participated in our passages and how he underwent phases of separation, liminality, and incorporation.

The last ten chapters are of surpassing value to all persons who are interested in investigating the relationship between the body, mind, and soul and those who have an appetite for using empirical phenomenon as a springboard to metaphysical realities and natural and sensory realities as a bridge to supernatural, extrasensory, and supersensory phenomenon. You will be introduced to parapsychological phenomenon, which are intrinsic in human personality and the commu- nity's life cycle and you will increase your knowledge of your deep structure and objective psyche of a particular people. Your self-knowledge and your ability to listen with a third ear and perceive with a third eye will be enhanced. You will be enticed into the habit of observing the invisible behind the visible, the unknowable behind the knowable, the supernatural behind the natural and discovering the meanings in rituals and myths.

a

CHAPTER TWO

What is Irua?

A. Definition

The name Gikuyu will be used for the tribe, language, country, and the founder of the tribe. Most writers, particularly those who are not Gikuyu use the name Kikuyu. All the Gikuyu when talking among themselves use the name Gikuyu. As we shall see later, the word Kikuyu is an incorrect transcription of the spoken word. I shall, therefore, employ the name Gikuyu throughout this book. The word Kikuyu will appear only when I am quoting other writers.

The English terms that have been used to define the Gikuyu puberty rite are initiation, circumcision, clitoridectomy, and labiadectomy. The term "initiation" is accepted and employed by the Gikuyus themselves. The terms clitoridectomy and labiadectomy are used by the missionaries and anthropologists. These terms imply that female circumcision involves excision of the clitoris and labia minora. The missionaries, particularly those who fueled the battle against female circumcision, preferred the term labiadectomy. They believed and tried to convince the world that the "brutal and barbarous custom" involved cutting off the labia minora and majora as well. This belief played an important role in shaping European strategies for dealing with the custom. The two terms, therefore, tend to distort the meaning and practice of the female puberty rite. The most appropriate and all embracing term is the Gikuyu word for the practice—irua. Irua, like Jewish circumcision, is merely bodily mutilation, which, however, is regarded as the conditio sine qua non of the whole teaching of tribal law, religion, and morality. The operation itself is embedded in a richly symbolic set of rituals. It is associated with much singing and dancing, and holds a profound significance for the initiates and their families. In this book, we shall, therefore, use the Gikuyu term irua. The English terms "initiation," "circumcision," and "puberty rite" will also be employed, but with the meaning of irua in mind.

It is also important to mention that the circumcision of boys and girls was not practiced by the Gikuyu only. It occurred among the Masai, Samburu, Nandi, Kipsigis, Githii, Embu, Kamba, and Taita of Kenya. However, the Gikuyu circumcision is our concern here. We shall, therefore, investigate its origin and the genesis of the Gikuyu tribe.

B. Origin of the Gikuyu

The Gikuyu derives from Mukuyu, a fig tree, literally meaning the people of the fig tree. According to our myth, Gikuyu, the founder of the tribe, came from the hole that was at the roots of a fig tree. This tree was in our "garden of Eden." Unlike the biblical garden of Eden, the Gikuyu garden of Eden really exists and its location is well known. This place of our origin is at Murang'a (the writer's District) in Central Province, North of Nairobi. This most sacred spot is known as Mukurwe Wa Gathanga, the tree of Gathanga.

As the legend has it, Ngai (the Great Provider) took Gikuyu from the roots of the fig tree to the peak of KereNyaga (the mountain of brightness and mystery), Mount Kenya, and showed him the beauty of the country, which he had given him. The country was so fertile with many rivers with clear cool water. It had a great forest of cedars, bamboos, olive trees, and many other trees, between which were small and large game. Far away to the south, there was a snowpeaked mountain, which is now called Mount Kilimanjaro. To the west was the mountain which is Nyandarua, and to the south the big hill called Kirima-Mbogo, "the hills of the buffaloes." With gratitude and great fear of the God-whoshines-in-Holiness, Gikuyu offered this prayer:

> O Great Provider, the Ancient of the Day God of Unique brightness, I have no word to thank you for thy ineffable wisdom and for thine priceless gift of the land. O Great Elder.

> Ruler of all things,

> I will be thine forever And will be ready to act in accordance with thy will.

After this prayer, Ngai blessed Gikuyu saying, "You, and your sons and daughters shall enjoy the beauty of the country and all its fruits. My blessing shall be with you and your offspring forever." After this, Ngai told Gikuyu to descend from the mountain and build his home in a place surrounded by Mikuyu, fig trees. Soon afterward, Ngai gave him a wife, Mumbi (the Creator), and they lived together happily and had nine daughters and no sons.

Gikuyu was disturbed because there were no sons who could marry his daughters. He prayed to God. God answered his prayer and told him, "Go, and take one lamb and kid from your flock. Kill them under the big tree near your homestead. Pour the blood and the fat of the two animals on the trunk of the tree. Then you and your family make a big fire under the tree, and there you will find nine young men who are willing to marry your daughters under any conditions that will please you and your family." Gikuyu did as he was commanded by Ngai. When he returned to the tree, he found nine handsome young men who greeted him warmly. He believed that they had come from God. Thus, the Gikuyu have a proverb, which says that, "Young men are God's gift." For a few moments, Gikuyu could not utter a word, for he was overwhelmed with joy. When he recovered from his emotional excitement, he took the nine youths to his homestead and introduced them to his family. The daughters accepted them as husbands, but under one condition, that the women should be the heads of the households and that they should all live together in the homestead of Gikuyu and Mumbi (Gikuyu's wife). All the Gikuyu believe that they are descendants of the nine daughters. They are all divided into nine clans that bear the names of the nine daughters: Wachera, Wairimo, Wamboi, Wangari, Wanjiro, Wangoi, Waithera, Warigia and Wanjiku.

As the myth has it, while women were holding a superior position in the community, they became domineering and ruthless fighters. They also practiced polyandry. Some men became angry and planned to overthrow the government. However, the women were taller and stronger than the men. Consequently, men held a secret meeting and resolved to seduce the leading women and their wives, and have sexual intercourse with them. After the meeting, men implemented their resolution. All women became pregnant and during the eighth month of their pregnancy, men overthrew their government and became the heads of the families. This was a bloodless revolution.

The Gikuyu tribe consists of three entities: (1) the family group (mbari) which brings together all those who are related by blood. That is a man and his wife, children, grand, and great-grandchildren; (2) The clan (muhiriga), which incorporates several mbaris. This is believed to have descended from nine daughters of Gikuyu and Mumbi; and (3) the age-group, which is formed during initiation. This is very important schooling for socialization, personality formation, for imparting the community's beliefs, values, and norms. It is a forum that helps an individual develop his social identity and a feeling of wholeness. The members of the age-group share personal experience and innermost feelings. They have a remarkable freedom of expression, and friendly confrontation. They discipline and train one another on how to live in a community as mature and moral persons. The biggest blow one might receive is to be ostracized by his or her age-group. (More about this in the section on "Sociological Perspective.")

While mbari and muhiriga systems help to form several groups of kinsmen within the tribe, , the system of age-grouping unites and solidifies the whole tribe in all the activities. As has been noted, the age-grouping is formed during circumcision. Thus, every year, the Gikuyu adolescents go through the initiation ceremony and automatically become members of one age-group regardless of the mbari, muhiriga, or district to which the individual belongs. They act as one body in all tribal matters and have a very strong bond of brotherhood and sisterhood among themselves. Hence, in every generation the Gikuyu tribal organization is stabilized by the activities of the age-group of old and young people who act harmoniously in its social, religious, and political life.

C. The Origin of Irua

The etymology of the word irua is unknown. According to one myth, when the daughters of Gikuyu married they had many children. Gikuyu, then, became a very prosperous and powerful king. Consequently, his government became autocratic and he compelled the people to leave their farms and join in tribal warfare. This caused people to be short of food, since they had no say in the administration of the country. Then Demi, the earliest known age-group, found that the easiest way to get rid of a despotic government was to have a system of peaceful revolutions every thirty to forty years. They then dethroned Gikuyu and made two rules that became law:

1. That all men should support the government by paying taxes and defending their country when there is war.
2. That every member of the community should be circumcised. Eventually, irua became the community rite par excellence and a phenomenon that brought the whole community together.

D. *The Initiates*

Since the irua was both a social as well as a physical puberty rite, the initiates were expected to have social and physical qualifications. Physically, a boy's puberty was established in the opinion of the public by the appearance of beard, underarm and pubic hair, the broadening of the shoulders, the thickening of the arms, the development of the male muscle patterns, and the deepening of the voice.

Girls' physical puberty was marked by an increase in height and weight. Unlike boys, girls were initiated during the earliest stage of their adolescence. This was because it was considered a taboo, for a girl to menstruate before or immediately after the initiation ceremony. If that happened, a diviner, was consulted so that she could be purified.

Socially, their parents or guardians should be in a good economic position. For that reason, the boys who were orphans were circumcised some years after their physical puberty. These boys could even be circumcised when they were twenty years of age. This did not apply to the girls.

The girls who had lost their parents were taken care of by relatives. So the ages of the girls who qualified for initiation ranged from nine to thirteen years, and the boys from fifteen to twenty years.

E. Preparation for Irua

The irua ceremony started with a dance known as mararanja. The word mararanja means to sleep in the yard of a homestead or away from the house. The entire community participated in this dance. Most of the songs were about sexuality. All the verbs and adjectives concerning sex and sexuality were learned at this occasion. The whole tribe acknowledged pubertal sexuality, which at this moment had reached its zenith. The adults became childlike by celebrating the dying childhood of the initiates. They were free to release their bad feelings that might have accumulated throughout the year. One was free to be as crazy as he liked, and whatever he did or said was allowed to go with the wind. Children were free to sleep away from home. There was a complete freedom of epression. People put on masks and painted their faces. The whole mararanja ceremony was marked with ecstasy. This ecstatic expression was common to most African people. Dr. Rottry, who comes from a different ethnic group, says this about his people: "Our forbearers knew this to be the case. So they ordained a time, once every year when every man and woman, free man and slave should have freedom to speak out just what was in their heads, to tell their neighbors just what they thought of them, and of their actions, and not only their neighbors, but also the king and chief."G. Parrinder. *West African Psychology(London; Lutterworth,1976)p33*

A few days before the irua, the initiates were put on a special diet. They were taught and prepared by their atiiri, sponsors. Then the elders celebrated a ceremony known as Kuraria Murungu, to sleep with and by God. The name Murungu refers to the God of our forefathers who is both transcendent and imminent. The ceremony was, therefore, considered as an act of communion with the ancestral God, whose protection was invoked to guide and protect the initiates through the forefathers. On the following day, there was another ceremony known as Kurathima Ciana, to bless the children, in which all the initiates were painted with white chalk called ira. This ira was obtained from Mount Kenya, the abode of the Gikuyu God. During the rite, the elders and the congregation sang antiphonally.

Peace be with children Beseech Ngai, peace, peace, peace.

The last preparatory ceremony was performed at the sacred tree. The initiates and the community gathered in the same place. A horn was blown and the boys ran about two miles to the sacred tree. They were followed by the girls. The boys climbed the tree and cut the leaves, while the girls gathered around singing and picking the leaves. The initiates ran back where they had left the elders. They ran with great excitement as though they were going to battle. This was considered the "fight between the spirit of childhood and adulthood." The boy who reached first was selected, there and then, as the leader of his age-group for life.

All the mararanja ceremonies were full of joy and excitement. As a Gikuyu Christian says, "I had attended many circumcision ceremonies in Fort Hall during the course of my stay at Karanja's home. They were festive occasions, full of excitement. I should say that I enjoyed them very much. The fact that I was Christian did not prevent me from enjoying these ceremonies."Mugo gatheru. A child of Two Worlds(Washington:Frederick A Praefer, 1957)p57

F. The Operation

When all the preliminary rites were performed, the initiates were ready for circumcision. The night before the surgery, the candidates did not sleep. Then at dawn, they proceeded to the river in the nude holding the sacred leaves, which they had taken from the Tree of God. They threw the leaves to the river. They then dipped themselves into the cold running water and stayed there for about half an hour.

With this done, they moved to the *irua* site.

If the boys and girls were to be circumcised on the same site, the boys usually lined up on the upper side, while the girls lined up at the lower side in front of the boys. A huge crowd of men, women, and children congregated around the initiate. Women and children stood in front of the candidates. Men stood at the rear. People joked and said that women enjoyed looking at the boys' full-grown penises.

The girls sat down with their legs wide open. Their sponsors sat behind them with their legs intertwined with those of the girls. The girls leaned against the sponsors while the latter held the shoulders of the former so as to prevent any physical movement during the operation. This stabilized the bodies of the initiates who were expected to sit stone-still without bodily movement or facial expression. After this preparation, the circumciser dashed at the initiates wearing ceremonial vestments, which were rich in ornaments. She wore dozens of earrings on each ear, dozens of necklaces, several bangles around her arms and ankles, and rattling bells on both legs. The attire and the ornaments made her appear extremely ceremonial and frightening. She then pulled out from her bag a well-sharpened blade and proceeded to perform surgery on each of the girls. With a stroke, she cut off the tip of the clitoris. As no other part of the girls' sexual organs were interfered with, this completed the girls' circumcisions. Most surgeons spent less than a minute on each surgery and for that reason, the unsuccessful initiates were very rare. In all the ceremonies that I attended when I was a boy, I never witnessed a coward candidate. The surgeon's knife produced a sharp pain as it cut through the prepuce. Since there was not any form of medical treatment, the pain persisted for about eight days. Thus, the painful experience that started during the circumcision day was just the beginning of the pain and ordeals.

Nevertheless, the initiates were being trained to confront pain with courage and accept it as a part of their earthly pilgrimage. They had to learn how to face suffering and how to deal with their fear in a creative manner. They learned to accept pain as a part of life. They demonstrated great courage during the most dreadful incident. Thus, any indication of fear during the cutting had a lifetime negative effect on the individual. The coward boys and girls were ridiculed by their peers since their failure was regarded as the failure of the whole group and of the parents and the sponsors. They bore an ineradicable social stigma throughout their lives.

Unlike the girls, the boys were not physically supported by their sponsor. Thus, after lining up in the nude, each boy dug holes with his heels and sat down with his legs open and his heels in the holes. The holes kept his legs in a steady position. He then folded his palms tightly in his fists. Pressing his thumbs tightly with the second and the third fingers, he put the fists on the right side of his neck like a boxer, looking either skyward or to the left side. As with the girls, he was not supposed to look at the circumciser. He had to sit still and not show any emotion or bodily movement—not even blink! When the boy was ready for a knife, the circumciser, who had no ornaments or vestments as the woman circumciser, held the full-grown penis, pulled the foreskin back and cut it off. Mugo Gathen says what he felt when he was cut. "It was very, very painful. But I did not show any feeling of fear or even act as if I were being cut. No medical aid was supplied first or after, and this made it extremely painful."(Achild of Two Worlds) p60-61 Despite the pain, there were very few failures. Most of the age sets had 100 percent success. That is, they all started the "school of wisdom" together, they all went through the ordeal and training together, and they were all awarded diplomas, which were not of papers, but the scars in the most precious parts of their bodies—the sexual organs.

After the cutting, one's ego was greatly strengthened and there was a feeling of success. The initiate felt that he had closed the river of childhood. He was on the side of the mature community. To use the words of Gatheru, "The cutting was over. I was now a mature Christian and a mature Gikuyu." I had the same feeling when I was cut. I felt the attainment of physiological and spiritual maturity. Spiritually, I had the same feelings as I had during the confirmation. I was conscious of being conjured to the cosmos and human communality. James Ngugi, in his *The River Between* described what happened to his main character, Waiyaki, when he was operated on. "The surgeon had done his work. Blood trickled freely on the ground sinking into the soil.

Henceforth, a religious bond linked Waiyaki to the earth, as if the blood was an offering. Around him, women were shouting and praising him. The son of Chege had proved himself!" The ritual bonded the individual not only to the creation, but also to the ancestral God, Murungu—the Being who stretches Himself over and beyond the cosmos and who existed before time and will continue to exist after time. They were introduced to spiritual pilgrimage. They had to move toward spiritual maturity. Their inner Tree of God was watered and fertilized.

Nudity, blood, meat, sex, community, and water are compelling psychic imagery among the Gikuyu and other African people. In dream, the imagery of nudity in public symbolizes the breaking of a taboo. A Gikuyu is trained from childhood to cover his private parts. It was and still is socially unacceptable to be in the nude in public. The only people who were permitted by the community to be in the nude were the mentally ill. Thus, during the cutting, the initiate not only had to endure pain, but had also experience shame. He/she had, as it were, to break an important law, in order that he/she may be introduced into an ethical and legal code in the manner that he/she will never forget. Blood and meat are imagery of death and life. If a Gikuyu dreams of eating meat, he believes that he will hear about death. Thus, the cutting of flesh and trickling of the blood symbolized death to childhood and new birth in adulthood.

Among the Gikuyu, as it is with the Africans, sex organs are the most sacred part of the body, which must always be covered as the Eucharistic elements. As we shall see later, there are ceremonial sexual acts in all the Gikuyu rites of passage. Thus, uncovering the holy elements in public was an awesome experience. Yet, one had to do unholy acts in order to be introduced to "fear of the holy" in the way which was complete. Sex organs are the most important part of the body for the Gikuyu and of course all human communities. And since initiation is the most significant rite, the initiates have to be marked on the most important, and most sensitive part of the body. For that matter, what was learned during the initiation was never forgotten.

After the surgeon had finished his or her job, the initiates were clothed by their sponsors. They were dressed in the white cloth, which passed through the right underarm and pinned or tied over the left shoulder. The cloth reached the ankle like an alb and was loose enough so as not to touch the wounded sexual organ. Led by their sponsors, the initiated walked slowly. They were followed by women who sung with jubilance in praising the initiates. They sung as though it was the initiates who were singing in them. They would, for instance, sing this way for Kamau's daughter:

> Tell Kamau I am cut. I'm feeling it.
> The fatted goat bring The black goat bring.
> The white goat bring.
> The red goat bring.
> The spotted goat bring.
> Tell Kamau I am cut.
> I'm feeling it.
> The fatted goat bring.

When the initiate reached the place of seclusion, the singing halted. Women who were singing disappeared. The initiates were then left with their sponsors and the senior advisor and his wife. In most cases, it was the senior advisor who hosted the initiates. He had to be a man full of knowledge, wisdom, and integrity. His wife was also expected to have similar qualifications. Both of them were called circumcisers. Their role, however, was not to perform surgery, but transmission of the whole gamut of the cultural ethos, which is known as the Gikuyu wisdom.

G. Seclusion

The initiates were then secluded in the homestead of a senior elder who might have had some of his children circumcised at this time. They were placed at the entrance of the homestead and were given delicious food. Meanwhile, the sponsors built for them a temporary training hut known as a githunu. This was built near the senior wife's girls' bedroom. The hut had two rooms, one of which was occupied by the male initiates and their sponsors and the other by the girl initiates and their sponsors. When the building of the hut was completed the fire was lit. All the areas, except the fireplace, were strewn with dry banana leaves, which served as bedding. This done, the initiates entered the hut in the evening. This was the beginning of practical training and education. Seclusion included the following:

1. Killing of the Circumcision Ram

This animal, which the women were singing about, was killed on the actual day of the operation while the lodge was being built and the initiates were resting and eating. The senior advisor, the owner of the homestead, provided an animal for sacrifice. This animal was slaughtered with a new knife, which had been provided for this special purpose. This ram, which was a sacrifice to God, was a symbol of the death of the initiates' childhood.

2. Submissiveness

The initiates, who were outnumbered by their sponsors and advisers, were expected to be humble and accept instructions without complaint. They had no freedom of arguing with their advisers. If the sponsors ordered them to go to the river to fetch water, they did that without a question. By surrendering to the sponsors, the initiates submitted to an authority, which was nothing less than that of the total community. They became like a *tabula rasa*, upon which the advisers and the sponsors inscribed the knowledge and wisdom of the tribe, in those respects, that pertained to their new status. Childish foolishness was removed. This was ritualized by the rite known as *kurutwo urimu na gutonywo matu* (to remove foolishness and pierce the ears). During this rite, the initiates knelt before the senior adviser and his wife, the wife took the new awl and a piece of root of the mucugucugu plant and symbolically pierced the earlobe of each candidate by passing these through the existing holes. This was an indication that the candidates' inner ears were now circumcised in order that they might hear and accept the wisdom of the tribe. Their heads were shaved so that new hair symbolizing the new wisdom might grow. Among other things, they were given sex education.

3. Sex Education

Since the Gikuyu regard virginity before marriage as something of fundamental importance, it was during this marginal period that the initiates were trained how to enjoy sexuality without breaking their virginity. The initiated girl was taught that when she accepted a young man for a date, she should not, under any circumstances, allow him to have full sexual intercourse with her, but only sleep with him and have gwiko ya nyondo—allow him to enjoy the warmth of her breasts. The initiate male was instructed that he should never, under any circumstances, attempt to have a full sexual intercourse with an initiated girl. He should never touch an uninitiated girl, even in fun, unless she was a member of his own family. He was advised not to have sexual intercourse with any man's wife, until he himself was married. In addition, he should not have a full sexual intercourse with an unmarried woman who may become his lover. But he was instructed on how to have ngwiko with her.

4. There was Ceremonial Sexual Intercourse

The senior adviser and his wife performed a ceremonial sexual intercourse on the first, third, fifth, and seventh days. This they did while all the initiates were present in the hut. As Leakey describes, "The muruithia climbed into the bed chamber of his wife, while she withdrew the wood from the fire so that it would not flame up and light the hut. In the darkness, she took off her cloak, hung it up, as usual, on the peg by her bed, and climbed into bed with her husband. They then had full sexual intercourse, and as soon as this had been achieved, the husband cleared his throat. This was a signal to the woman on duty outside that the "sacrifice" of sexual intercourse was "over." This was a symbolic action indicating that the initiates have been born into the world of sexuality and productivity.

5. During the Seclusion the Initiates were Fed

The sponsors put the girls' food on a banana leaf, which served as a plate. The leaf was lifted to the mouth without the girl actually touching its contents with her hands. The same thing was done for the males. The only thing that the initiates were allowed to touch with their hands was meat, since the Gikuyu never regarded meat as food (irio). The feeding signified the newness of life—the initiates were newcomers in the adult community.

6. The Initiates were Given a Special Honor and Blessing

During this painful occasion, the parents and relatives brought them special gifts. They were also honored and blessed by the senior adviser and his wife. This act, which is known as "the rite of honoring the initiates," consisted of making a movement with the body that was rather like a jerky bow while bringing the hands up in front of the face and down again the staff of office being all the time in both hands. These blessings were reciprocal. The Gikuyu believe that when a parent blesses his child, the parent receives the blessing from the child as well. Some parents could even regard one of their children as a "lucky bird." My wife, who was her father's "lucky bird" tells me that her father, who was a business man, could not come out of bed before receiving a blessing from her. Her father believed that through his daughter's blessing, he could have a good day, have more customers, and make more money. So in this rite of bowing to the children, the initiates were symbolically taught how to give and receive the blessings.

7. The Shooting of Rats and Working in the Garden

In this rite, the male sponsors made bows and arrows. They then made a small clearing in the homestead and put some corn to attract rats and mice. When the rats came, the sponsors shot them with their arrows. After killing one rat, the sponsors shouted, then the boys rushed as though they were raiding enemies. They then stood near the dead rat and shot it. This act symbolized the killing of the enemies, and it was an indication of the transition from boyhood to warriorhood. Meanwhile, the girls were taken out by female sponsors to the neighboring gardens and were made to go through the act of planting, weeding, and harvesting. They were then taken to the bush where they collected firewood and took it to the initiation mother. When they reached her, they were given a small bottle of castor oil. They then waited to receive and applaud the warriors who returned triumphantly from "cattle raiding." This ritual was more of a division of labor. More about this is in the section on "Sociological Perspective."

8. Going to the Tree of God

As we have noted, the name Gikuyu derives from Mukuyu, the fig tree. For the Gikuyu, therefore, the Mukuyu is more than a sacred tree. It is a totem, which makes them conscious of their origin and reminds them of the totality of their ontology. Being a Gikuyu, I have to admit, that even now, it would be an awesome experience to be alone at night under the Mukuyu. To go back to the point, the marginal period includes the rite under the tree. The senior adviser took beer and poured it under the tree; took some honey, which he smeared on it; and then he prayed to Murungu, the ancestral God. He then took the milky juice from the tree and marked the male initiates on their cheeks, around their eyes, on the center of their foreheads, and on their hands and legs. Then, the wife of the senior adviser put the milky juice on both of the girls' temples, on their necks, on both of their nipples, and on their hands. Symbolically, this rite connected the initiates with the Great Tree out of which the Gikuyu, the father of the tribe, came. The initiates were attached to the tribe's primordial time and ancestral God, who is both transcendent and imminent. We shall discuss more about the Tree in Chapter Thirteen.

H. Incorporation

There are three terms which were used for this phase,s Gutonyio(to be entered),r guciarwo (to be born) and inukia (bringing home). The three terms, which were used in different localities, are not contradictory. They all express the meaning of the rite, which are being entered and born into a new life, a home-coming after being away in seclusion.

This rite was performed in the evening of the ninth (Kenda) day after the end of mararanja, when the herds and flocks of the homestead came home for the night. The word kenda (nine) means it is in the womb. It symbolizes the nine months in which the fetus remains in the womb. Kenda is a birthday. Since the Gikuyu consists of nine clans, the number nine is a symbol of perfection and wholeness. So, performing the rite on the ninth day meant being born at the opportune time and to wholeness of life.

The ceremonies included sacrificing an animal and eating meat, pigeon peas, and bananas, and drinking millet gruel and beer. All these are ceremonial foods and drinks. The parents of the first born were given brass earrings as a sign of seniority. They moved from the state of young adulthood to mature adulthood.

The final rite, which ended all irua rites, was concluded by a ceremonial sexual act. At night, the initiates who were in nyumba (the symbol of fertility) slept in the girls' bedroom. The parents waited until the initiates and children were asleep and then they had ceremonial sexual intercourse twice. This demonstrated that the initiates were now born into a sexual world.

a

CHAPTER THREE

The Ritual Context

In this chapter we will view the Gikuyu initiation within the context of the totality of the Gikuyu life cycle. As we will see, the initiation was the water-shed between all preadolescent rites and post-adolescent rites. These rites of passage included birth, marriage, middle adulthood, retirement, and death rites. All pre-pubertal rites anticipated the great occasion of the irua, while post-pubertal rites looked back to it. The birth rites, as we have noted, were the beginning of the preparation of irua.

A. *The Birth Rites*

The African people, have a great admiration for children. Both male and female children are equally appreciated. Traditionally, after realizing that she had missed two menstrual periods, a woman considered that she was pregnant and informed her husband of her conception. The husband responded by having regular sexual intercourse for two months in order to promote the growth of the child in the womb. After four months of pregnancy, genital sexual intercourse was replaced by another type of sexual enjoyment known as ngwiko—the couple sleeping together, facing each other with their legs interwoven, and fondling each other, rubbing their breasts together and engaging in love-making conversation.[1] Ngwiko art and rules were learned during and after the irua ceremonies, so initiation was necessary for successful pregnancy and delivery. Birth took place in the homestead.

The Gikuyu homestead included Thingira (the husband's house) and several Nyumbas (wives' houses) depending on the number of wives. The husband and male visitors spent most of their times in Thingira; the mother, children, and women visitors occupied the nyumba. The birth took place in the mother's house at Kweru (the newness). When the woman realized that her time for giving birth was near, she did not go far from Nyumba, but remained in the homestead doing light work such as cooking, sweeping, and sewing leather garments. When her labor pain started, all the children (except the oldest, initiated unmarried daughter) were sent out. Children either went to the house of their step-mothers or to their father's house. Then women who assisted the midwife lit a large fire of dry wood in the hearth in the center of the house. The fire was kept burning in order to provide adequate illumination. The fire symbolized life and presence of the Great Provider—Ngai. Meanwhile, the expectant mother, facing Mount Kenya, held the two bars at Kweru with both hands while the midwife's assistant supported her in the position, which the Gikuyu regarded as the best for childbirth, that is, with the legs wide apart and knees slightly flexed so that the body was in a semi-crouching position. One of the assistants stood behind the woman and put her arms around the woman's chest while pressing the small of the woman's back gently with her knees. In this manner, the pelvis was kept at the angle, which was considered best for delivery.

Immediately after birth, the child was washed with cold water—an action which is repeated for its symbolic meaning during initiation. The cold water was supposed to make the baby cry. A cry was an indication that the baby was mature and healthy. After this, the helping women made a ceremonial shout known as ngemi. The delivering mother did not scream as John S. Mbiti suggests, neither did she ululate as L.S.B. Leakey tells us. Ngemi is neither a scream nor an ululation. It is a ceremonial, joyous, and appreciational shout or song that is uttered as follows: a-a-a-a-a-ri-ri-riri…ri. Ngemi evokes a profound feeling. The women said five ngemis for a baby boy and four for a girl. The number of shouts did not imply a preference, but a declaration of the sex and the name of the child.

The ngemi was the cue for the father, who at this time was either in his house or near the delivery house. He came to the doorway and asked with a loud voice, "Whom have you seen?" (Muona uu). The answer depended on whether the baby was a boy or girl. If it was the firstborn son the answer was, "We have seen men and it is your father." For the second born son, they answered, "We have seen men and it is your father-in-law." In the case of the first born daughter, they replied, "We have seen women and it is your mother." If the child was the second born daughter the correct answer was, "We have seen women and it is your mother-in-law." After this, all other children were named alternately after the husband's brothers and sisters and his brothers-in-law and sisters-in-law. Diagram number one clarifies this point.

As with irua, the birth of the child brought the community together. During the acknowledgement of the sex and the name, it was asserted that the child was born into a community. The baby boy was born as one of the "men" and the girl as one of the "women." The birth was the focal point of those who were alive and the living-dead. As Mugambi and Kirima write, "A successful birth was held to be due to the propitiation of God, spirits, and ancestors, and the favorable attitude of the mother to everyone and the skills of the midwife."[4]

Like the initiates, the mother and the child were secluded for several days. Meanwhile, the mother was tended to by other women who gave her fermented gruel and soft food. After seclusion, the husband slaughtered a goat or a sheep as a sacrifice to God. Some meat was boiled and eaten by the family and neighbors. Some was kept to be used by the mother. After this, the father went to the garden and brought bananas, yams, and sugarcane (men's crops) and gave them to the mother and the baby. This was a symbolic action, which demonstrated the father's love and appreciation for the mother and the child. This rite was followed by itega. That is, the neighbors brought food, gruel and firewood to the family of the newly born baby. Itega was also a community banquet. Thus, the birth rite commenced with the community and was concluded by the community.

As noted, irua dominated the behavior of the expectant woman and the community which awaiting the birth of the child. Like the irua ceremony, the woman was expected to endure pain. She was expected to groan courageously, but she should neither scream nor cry. As Mugambi and Kirima write, "The mother was expected to endure labor patiently. Girls were trained for this even in the rites of passage at puberty, where qualifying in the test of courage required the patient enduring of pain, a young child was taught that crying at childbirth could kill the child—crying on this occasion would put her mother and mother-in-law to shame."[5] So, as in initiation, the labor pain had to be endured in patience.

B. *The Weaning Rites*

Customarily, a Gikuyu woman avoided conception until the child whom she was sucking was between two to three years. In most cases, children weaned themselves, because once they started to eat more ordinary foods, they ceased to want their mother's milk, which was depleted. Sometimes, a child went on sucking so long that his/her mother decided that it had to be forcibly weaned. This she did by rubbing snuff on her nipples; this quickly cured the child of any desire to suck.

Immediately after the weaning, the father and the mother arranged for the weaning rites. If the child was a boy, the father took him to the field, made a small bow and arrow and helped the boy to throw the arrow. The baby girl was taken to the forest by her mother who made her a bundle of firewood and helped the little girl to carry them on her back. This rite, as irua, began to define the labor roles. The boy was made aware that he was growing into manhood and would be obliged to defend his country. The girl was prepared to be a woman who would be responsible for nyuma— the house.

C. Rebirth

The rebirth rite is as significant as circumcision, for without it, a child was regarded as incomplete and as merely an extension of the mother's personality. If he was a boy, he could not sleep in the father's house with other boys who had undergone through the rite. He has to sleep with the mother in her house. Customarily, if the child died before the rebirth, the corpse was never buried, but was taken by the mother to a bush. His body became a meal for a hyena. The mother disposed of the body as she would do to the fetus his nourishment. He was, as it were, tutored on how to draw from the environment. He no longer merely depended on his biological self, but he grew to a whole by drawing from the environment. Thus, what he was and what he was to become was inborn, given, and acquired. He had to be his ancestors, his parents, his extended family, his neighborhood, his environment, and his self-determination.

The use of the leaves from the sacred tree was intended to give a chid a cordial relationship with holy objects and the ancestral God, who was conceived as the Great Provider, the Ancient of the Day, the Transcendent and Immanent Being who shines in holiness. The child could now grow spiritually. He had to become a part of a large worshipping community. In addition, the rebirth symbolized physical birth. This is why the mother and the child had to be in the nude. The nude child had to be pushed to its mother's genitalia. But birth had to take place at an age when the child could always remember the occasion. The child entered into the conscious experience of his/her birth, the beginning of the sasa (now) period. The rite terminated the child's babyhood, and brought him/her to the gate of full participation in the life of the society. Now the child was ready to enter the stage of initiation, and to be fully incorporated to the activities and responsibilities of corporate manhood and womanhood. The ceremony also symbolized the fact that he/she was born again to carry on the ancient fire, which meant to perpetuate the Gikuyu tradition. The rite qualified the child for initiation and the initiation paved the way for marriage.

D. *The Marriage Rite*

Initiation and all other preceding rites were preparations for marriage. The Gikuyu marriage, like those of other African people, was a complicated matter with economic, social, and religious aspects. It had many complex ceremonial rites attached to it; thus, for our purpose we can only telescope the procedure and meaning of the rites.

After choosing partners, the young man and woman reported to their parents, the parents informed the relatives and neighbors, eventually the dowry was taken to the parents of the bride, and then the wedding day was announced. In all these stages there were ceremonial rites. The ceremonial elements that were used included beer, meat, grain, and other food stuffs.

Marriage was a focus of existence. It was a point where all the members of the given community met the departed, the living, and those yet to be born. All the dimensions of time met here and the whole drama of history was repeated, reviewed, and revitalized. Those who were not circumcised were not qualified for marriage. In the Gikuyu's eyes, one who does not marry was not only abnormal, but also subhuman. Marriage meant procreation, perpetuation of life, social status, and attaining a state of manhood and womanhood. Marriage was a religious duty and a responsibility for everyone. The irua prepared youth and gave them freedom for marriage.

E. The Rite of the Middle Adulthood

As it has been noted, the initiation of the first born was a rite of passage for the parents. According to the Kamba tribe, after initiation the parents of the candidate had ritual sexual intercourse on the third and seventh nights. According to the Gikuyu, the senior adviser to the initiates and his wife had ceremonial sexual intercourse on the first, third, fifth and seventh day. This was a symbolic action, indicating that both the initiates and parents have moved to another stage of life. As we have seen, there was a special rite that was performed after the healing of the wounds. At this ceremony, the parents were provided with brass earrings as a sign of seniority. This was done when the firstborn was initiated. The parents qualified to be elected as Athuri a Kiama (literally, miraculous elders), "the ruling council." The members of this council were also sacrificing elders.

F. *The Rite of Handing-Over Authority*

The Gikuyu word "ituika," which is used for this rite means a landslide, and its verb tuika means to slide or to break. Ituika is, therefore, a rite of passage in which the authority of the older generation is expected to "land-slide" and move toward the valley of the living dead. As Permenas Githendu Mockerie points out, ituika is "a system which has been used among the Kikuyu by every new generation when it desires to relieve the old generation form the administration of the country."[8] It was a rite of handing-over authority from one generation to the next.

The Gikuyu myth connects the origin of ituika with irua. The ituika was established by Ndemi, the earliest known age group, the first Gikuyus to be circumcised. As we have noted, it was Ndemi who dethroned the King Gikuyu. After this, they made two laws. One of these laws was that every member of the community should be circumcised. The next thing that Ndemi did was to establish ituika. It resolved that all circumcised men and women are equal, and in this way denounced the status of a king.

The ituika did not have complicated ceremonies. The incoming generation presented goats (for the Gikuyu, goats are the most precious of gifts) to the outgoing generation. The goats were sacrificed at the sacred grove and then feasted on. Immediately after the feast the old generation relinquished its social and political powers and responsibilities to the young generation. The meaning and the purpose of ituika were respect and honor for the older generation. The accomplishment of the passing generation was celebrated. During this time, the old generation recognized and blessed the new one. As with irua, ituika facilitated democracy in that during the ceremony, the people elected their leader and the ruling council. Thus, "the ituika system not only gave the kikuyu democratic ideas, but also provided full liberty for every citizen to express his opinion."[9] During the ituika the elderly people were made aware that they were land- sliding to Menengai, the abode of the living-dead.

G. Death Rites

"To die is not to perish." This is a famous Gikuyu saying that portrays their attitude toward death. Even though death is perceived with a considerable degree of fatalism and was never in any ordinary circumstance welcomed, the Gikuyu did not have the haunted fear of death, which grips the people of many civilizations. Although the bereaved expe rience a great loss, they rarely weep publicly. I have celebrated many funerals among the Gikuyu, most of which were attended by hundreds of people, but I scarcely saw tears. I also witnessed a positive attitude in my maternal grandfather, Gatungu, when he was nearing his death. Whenever I visited him, he used to say, "John, I am awaiting for my passport to go to Menengai." The grandfather was calmly waiting for the day when Ngai (God) will call him to Menengai (a place near Nakuru Town, Kenya) the abode of the living-dead.

As with irua, a Gikuyu who knew that his end was near, usually faced the fact patiently and with equilibrium. This was partly because he had learned during circumcision to accept pain, and partly because there was no idea of hell. The life of the living-dead was not unpleasant, for his needs were met by those members of the family who remained on earth. The dying person also believed that in Menengai, he had a spiritual body, cattle, sheep, goats, a farm, and better still, that he would be in the community. It was also believed that the day of one's death was predetermined by God at birth, and for this reason, there was no need for unduly mourning or worrying about it. Paradoxically, the departed was far away at Menengai, yet he or she was near the family's homestead.

When one died, the type of funeral was determined by initiation. Broadly speaking the Gikuyu had two ways of disposing of the body—by burying it in a grave or by putting it (kibirira-ini) in the graveyard and leaving it there to be taken by a hyena. Only those who had initiated sons who were buried. The bodies of the rest were carefully placed at the Kibirira-ini. Many complex ceremonial rites were performed before and after the disposal of the body. For our purpose, we will discuss one of the rites known as hukura. Since there were many types of hukura, we shall concentrate on the hukuka for the elder who had initiated sons.

The word hukuka means to unbury and has the same root with the word huko—mole rat—an animal which is notorious for burying objects. The aim of huruka was not to unbury the body, but to release the soul and its transference to the place of the spirits and to remove the contagion of death, so to enable all members of the family to resume normal life once again. It took place when the moon reached the same place it had been when the burial took place (interval of 28 days). The whole ceremony took eight days.

On the first day, the ram known as ndurume ya gikuu (the ram of death) was slaughtered and its meat was eaten by all those who took part in the ceremony. Meanwhile, all the widows, except the senior wife, elected male partners known as endia njora (the sellers of the swords, the swords being penises), for performing ceremonial sex acts. After eating the meat and drinking the beer, the widows and their partners put on rings made of creeping grass known as igoka. This was followed by a ceremonial sex act. It started with the senior wife and the young brother of the dead husband. As soon as this was completed, the man cleared his throat loudly to give cue to the elders in the courtyard. When the elders heard this signal, they told the second widow and her "sword seller" to start the ceremonial sexual intercourse. The same procedure was followed until all the widows had performed the act. This act, which concluded the ceremony of the first day was known as gutheca gikuu—literally to pierce death, metaphorically, it means to have sexual intercourse with death. Symbolically, death was conquered by fertility.

All the unmarried children of each widow should be present in the hut when this rite is being performed, for the mother was doing this not only for herself, but on behalf of all her unmarried children. The widows slept with their partners for eight days and had sexual intercourse twice every night except the second, fourth and sixth nights, which were known as mutiro—the occasion for suspending the normal activities. The second day was a day of complete rest. Sexual intercourse among the widows and their partners was suspended. The animals of the deceased were segregated according to their sex during the entire period of the hukura ceremony so they might not mate. On this day, all those who were in the ceremony did nothing but eat, sit, and sleep on the courtyard. This was a day of complete relaxation.

On the third day, the widows and their partners had their heads shaved. The widows anointed their chests, arms, shoulders, knees and feet with castor oil. The rite was concluded with ceremonial sexual intercourse. The fourth day, as the second day, was a day full of rest. On the fifth day, the hukura ceremony entered into a second stage. While the first four days were known as "bad days" the next four, beginning on the fifth day were "good days." The aim of the ceremonies now was to return to normal life. On this day, the elders slaughtered a he-goat known as thenge ya gutiira (the supporting goat) and its meat was eaten by all the members of the family and the "sword sellers." While the rite was concluded with ceremonial sexual intercourse, the order of seniority was no longer observed, provided each widow and her partner had sexual intercourse twice.

On the sixth day, all those who had been engaged in hukura washed in the running rivers, drank beer known as njohi ya guthambia moko (the beer for washing the hands) and ate meat of a stall-fattened animal. Since this was a mutiro day (the day of rest) there was no ceremonial sex act. On the seventh day, the elder brother, half-brother, or patrilineal cousin of the deceased brought a fattened ram and beer, which was feasted on by all the family, relatives, and neighbors. This feast was more of a family reunion and it marked the end of contamination. Since the Gikuyu regarded seven as an unlucky number, there was no sexual intercourse.

On the eighth day, the diviner did the final purification of the widows and their partners. Once again, that night they slept together and had sexual intercourse twice. This ended the hukura rites and on the following day, people resumed normal life. The partners of the widows received the fee for which they sold their swords, which were either goats or sheep, and then went home.

If during the hukura ceremony one of the partners developed an affectionate relationship with his partner, that man had a special right to come and have sexual intercourse with her and even beget children with her. But these children would belong to the deceased man and would be cared for by the relative who inherited the widow.

The reader cannot fail to see a remarkable resemblance between the irua rites and death rites. The ritual life cycle of the individual continually uses the symbols of death and rebirth. From irua onward, rebirth is associated with sexuality. As a sacrament, sexual intercourse ensures the rebirth of the deceased. To give another example of rebirth through sexuality, the first born son is given his father's father's name and so on. At the same time, the rebirth of the first child causes the parents to be reborn as young adults, while the initiation of the first born causes them to be reborn as mature adults. As Van Gennep(in Rites of Passage) has pointed out, rites of passage often involve death and rebirth.

Unlike irua, death did not involve the entire community. It only brought together the family and relatives and those who were closely connected with the deceased. The significance of irua lies on the fact that it exerts enormous influence on the Gikuyu personality from birth to death. As we have noticed, irua was a criterion for the type of burial rites. It was only a circumcised son who dug the grave and carried the body of his deceased father to the grave. For this reason, he who had no initiated son was not buried.

Moreover, when an unborn-again child died, its body was carried by its mother alone to the graveyard. That was so because the child was regarded as a part of its mother, rather than an individual member of the community. The irua qualified one to live and die as a member of the community.

a

Part Two

CHAPTER FOUR

Clinical Reflection

a. As it has been noted in Chapter One, irua externalized and ritualized the adolescents' psychological and sociological conflicts. In this chapter, we shall use irua as an observation post, which will help us to observe what actually happens in the bodies of the adolescents. It will also help us to penetrate the adolescents' inner world, and give us a wider and deeper understanding of their social conflicts. We shall see how the irua ritualized the tension caused by conflicting demands from parents and the peer groups, the gap between what he is and what is expected of him by society. It is hoped that by conceptualizing the irua metaphor with these disciplines, we shall illumine the adolescents' world and, thus, be able to minister to them more effectively.

A. *Physiological Perspectives*

b. Physiology is defined as the science or the branch of biology dealing with the functions of the living organism or its parts. The term derives from a compound Greek word physiliqia. The first part of the word, physia, means nature; the second part logos, means discourse, reason, or science. Hence, in this section, we shall view the irua in the light of the function of the adolescents' physical organism. We shall conceptualize the irua in the light of what actually happens in the bodies of the adolescents.

2. At the onset, the terms "adolescence" and "puberty" should be distinguished. The word adolescence refers to the transitional period be tween puberty and adulthood. Biologically, an adolescent is a boy or girl in his or her teenage years. The word puberty, on the other hand refers to the state of physical development in which persons are capable of begetting or bearing children. In botany, the term puberty is used to refer to the period when a plant first begins to bear flowers. In a deeper sense, puberty is a process of physical maturation, which produces secondary sex characteristics and leads to fertility. In contrast, adolescence is better described as a process of psychological and social maturation, which leads to full citizenship. Puberty begins in a person's early teens (to some girls it may begin at the age of ten) and ends a few years later; adolescence begins with puberty and may last a decade or more. As it has been noted, there is a distinction between physical puberty and social puberty.

a. Some authorities divide puberty into three stages— pre-puberty, puberty, and post puberty. *Pre-puberty* is that stage before the child starts developing any preliminary characteristics of sexual maturation. This period is characterized by a spurt in physical growth and the beginning of primary and secondary characteristics. *Puberty* is the period in which the generative organs become capable of functioning and the secondary sex characteristics become highly evident. This, however, does not mean that the boy or girl is capable of reproduction. The third stage, *post-pubescence* is a one or two year span of adolescence. During this time, most of the skeletal growth is completed and the new biological functions become fairly well established.

b. It should be emphasized, however, that adolescence cannot be divided arbitrarily into three stages any more than the entire growth process can be broken down into sharply defined steps of development. Nevertheless, adolescence is a period of enormous growth and constant change. During this stage, the psychological responses of the individual are directly influenced by the particular aspects of physical growth that are in the ascendancy. The physical changes increase conflicts for the individual, which were ritualized by the irua.

c. As mentioned, during the mararanja (the first phase of the irua) one was free to be as crazy as he liked. This was the externalization and ritualization of the feelings of the adolescents, which were partly caused by the following physiological factors.

3. The adolescents are bothered by the *increase of height and weight.* During puberty, an average girl grows two to four inches and gains eight or

ten pounds a year. The average boy gains twelve to fourteen pounds and grows four to five inches. Because of this growth, boys and girls begin to feel unfamiliar with their bodies. They feel awkwardness. They see their heads being so far away from their feet. The increase of height and weight in both sexes results in a greater intake of food. While American society, which emphasizes slenderness, would make the adolescent feel guilty because of his weight, in Africa they are made to feel guilty because of "eating too much." The irua lessened this problem in that during and after seclusion, the adolescents were expected to eat as much as they liked and be as fat as possible.

a. The adolescents are disturbed by either being too short or too tall. Traditionally, the Gikuyu boys and their parents were harassed for shortness. The girl with a flat chest who was taller than her peers was also harassed. In addition, the adolescents experienced tension because of *motor awkwardness.* This is caused by an uneven growth of muscles and bones. Boys and girls who are unusually awkward in motor skills necessary to play the sports or games of their peers feel inferior. The experience of skin eruptions, the new awareness of perspiration, and body odors upset the majority of teenagers.

Adolescents are unfamiliar with and troubled by the growth of the primary and secondary sex organs. Boys worry about the size of their penises. They wonder whether they are normal or not. The influence of Puritanism and docetic Christianity in Africa makes boys feel guilty of their wet dreams. They feel sinful because of their uncontrollable erections. Girls are disturbed by their pubic and auxiliary hair and by their first menstruation, because it is a new experience. Worse than that, traditionally, menstruation is regarded as impure. As mentioned earlier, if a girl menstruates before the initiation, she must be ritually purified by a diviner. Influenced by this belief, a Gikuyu girl may consider herself impure during her period and, therefore, excuse herself from taking the Eucharist. It is during their seclusion that girls were taught about their periods. There is an interesting story about an urban Christian girl who went to the countryside to be initiated. During the seclusion, the initiates were given sex education The sponsors employed dialogical methods. A story is told of a dialogue between a sponsor and a city girl. The sponsor posed a question: "Is there anyone among you who has seen the moon (the Gikuyu word for moon, mweri, means moon, month, and menstruation)?"

"Yes," answered the city girl. "I do see the moon in the sky every month."

"It is not that moon," replied the sponsor. "I am asking whether you have seen the blood."

"Yes," answered the city girl. "I have been washed by the blood of Jesus."

The sponsor then became aware that the girl did not understand "the moon." She then explained to the girl and other initiates what is "the moon" and what they should do when it comes. There are physiological reasons for tension during the first and even future menstruations. As the extra lining of the uterus is deteriorating, particularly just before menstruation, some girls and women experience unpleasant symptoms. These can include fatigue, headaches, abdominal cramps, tenderness in the breast, and an increase in pimples and moodiness.

Another cause of conflict is the *unevenness of the rate of sexual maturation for both sexes*. During some period in their middle to late teens, most boys have a sex drive that is stronger than it will ever be again. During this time they become erect very easily and desire orgasms often. This decreases as they get older. In contrast, most girls do not feel an intense drive until later in their lives. Often, the peak of a woman's sex drive is not reached until she is well into her 30s or 40s. Thus, while a teenage boy may feel guilt because he is "oversexed," the girl may feel guilty because she is "undersexed." This will be discussed in the section on "Psychological Perspective" and "Sociological Perspective."

B. Psychological Perspective

In this section, we will look at the irua from the viewpoint of Jean Piaget, Sigmund Freud, and Erik H. Erikson. It is illuminating to look at the irua from the perspective of Jean Piaget's personology. Piaget put the intellectual developmental process into four main chronological periods. The order of succession in this process is consistent, although the age at which different stages are attained may vary somewhat depending on the child's motivation, practice, and cultural differences. In this schema, it is the fourth period, which is relevant to our study. Piaget regarded this period, which begins in early adolescence, as the period of formal operation. During this stage, an individual lives in both the present and the non-present. He is no longer merely concerned with the real, but also is concerned with the possible. In committing himself to the possible outcome of a situation, he thinks beyond the present. While the child is incapable of theorizing or building systems, the adolescent builds systems and theories.

While this book disagrees with Piaget's emphasis on chronology, his theory has insightful points. As we have seen, it is during the period of adolescence that the irua imparted formal knowledge. After the initiation, one was expected to live in accordance with conventional expectations and requirements. The traditional man gave theories to an individual when he was capable of theorizing. Piaget identifies the adolescent's tension, which we have discussed in a previous section. The tension is caused by the fact that the adolescent lives between present and non-present. His world of childhood is no longer real; his adult world is not fully attained.

Sigmund Freud can also shed light on our understanding of the irua. Freud is one of the founding fathers of depth psychology and the originator of psychoanalysis. Unlike Piaget's psychology, which was born out of the university laboratory in an attempt to investigate theoretical questions on normal subjects, psychoanalysis stemmed from the medical clinic and from the attempt to help patients to live more normal lives. As Raymond J. Corsin rightly contends that psychoanalysis is the oldest and most influential of all personality theories. Psychoanalysis is relevant to our discussion of the irua because of its discovery of the primitivity of humanity and the power of the sexual drive (libido). For Freud, the primitive end of the spectrum has biologicallybased instincts known as *id*. This is that part of us which enjoys and longs for antistructure. It listens to and obeys our instincts. At the other end of the spectrum, there is that part which strives to harmonize instinctive gratification with moral standards. This is known as *super-ego*. In between, there is *ego*, which attempts to balance id and super-ego.

Ego strives for sophistication and a more structured reality-based element. The reader cannot fail to see how the irua externalizes and ritualizes the "primitive" aspect of humanity. All the Gikuyus, young and old, longed for mararanja (just as Americans long for Mardi Gras), an occasion, which gave every individual freedom to be unstructured. We were to articulate all our dreams and fantasies.

Freud, not only discovered the force of sexual drive, but he also regarded the psychosexual constitution and certain noxiae in the sexual life as the most important causes of neurotic disorder. According to Freud, puberty is often, but not always, stormy. The storm is caused by the fact that the repressed sexual feelings of childhood are intensified. Previous defenses are no longer adequate and sweeping readjustment is required. This becomes complicated since the adolescents cannot go back to earlier dependent infantile states. The reactions to this behavior are varied and range from flagrant, rebellious, antisocial, and promiscuous behavior to the seeking of ascetic ideas and the pursuit of a monastic life. In a sense, what Freud says here is true to my personal experience. Owing to the turmoil of my early adolescence, I became a leader of a street gang that engaged in various types of antisocial behavior. When I was fifteen, I gave my life to Christ. When I was eighteen, I was motivated by the dynamism of adolescence and the power of the Holy Spirit and, thus, preached the Gospel in an unbalanced manner. I preached at the market place, bus stations, railway stations, shopping centers, and in hospitals, prisons, police lines, offices, bars, and hostels. My feet stepped on all the locations in Nakuru Town. I preached to the Africans, Asians, and Europeans. I became the most famous adolescent in the town. My visiting hours were as awkward and stormy as my adolescence. At one time, I visited a European family at dawn. I knocked at the door and a man let me in. The family was taking their breakfast. The man who was so astonished by seeing a black teenager with a Bible, asked, "What can I do for you?"

I replied, "I have come to tell you that Jesus loves you, but hates sin."

"But it is too early," he exclaimed.

"No," I replied. "It isn't too early, because you do not know whether he is coming this morning or in the afternoon." After a short homily, I bade them goodbye. I was full of joy. In spite of my awkwardness, the Spirit seemed to enjoy blowing me whenever he wanted. The question that used to fuel my joy was, "Are you mad?" I excessively read the Bible with a group of boys; we read ten chapters a day with the intention of reading the whole Bible. During these stormy years, I acquired a spirituality that I shall never lose.

This author, therefore, agrees with Freud that an adolescent can never maintain an optimal balance.

He is either delinquent or a monk. However, I do not agree that the major cause of the storm is the repressed sexual feelings of childhood. One also misses the boat by assuming that all children of all cultures suffer from an Oedipus complex and a castration fear. As we have seen, the Gikuyu child was a part of his mother until he was born again with a goat. The second birth took place during pre-adolescence. The mother and the children lived in nyumba while the husband lived in a separate hut. The parents did not fondle each other in the presence of their children. They waited for children to go to bed, after which either the father went to nyumba or the wife went to thingira. They then enjoyed sexual interplay. For this reason, there was no room for the atmosphere that could create an Oedipus complex. Furthermore, the irua minimized this complex in that after the initiation, the young men lived in a separate hut.

It is very illuminating to view the irua from the perspective of Erik H. Erikson, one of the most popular and unusual personologists of our century. Unlike other psychoanalysts, he became a psychoanalyst without a medical degree. He taught in the universities without academic degrees. Unlike Fraud, Erikson de-emphasized psychosexual and stressed psychosocial aspects of the personality. He cared less about id and super-ego and focused on ego identity. His theory of personality development, for which he is best known, is very relevant to this book. Basing his ego psychology on the rites of passage of the American Indians, Erikson theorized that an individual goes through eight developmental stages.

These stages may not be determined chronologically. Our initiates come under the fourth and fifth stages.

Erikson terms the fourth stage "industry versus inferiority." In this stage, the child either becomes industrious or suffers from inferiority feelings. At this stage children receive some systematic instruction. In preliterate-people (as the traditional Gikuyu), much is learned from adults who become teachers and perhaps the greater amount is learned from older children. As we have seen, the initiates were taught by the senior advisor and their sponsors during the healing of their wounds. After this, they were left alone to confront and help each other to assimilate the adult's teachings. In addition, they were taught by their senior age-group. According to Erikson, it was at this stage that the children learned to handle utensils, tools, weapons, and to become potential providers. As I have indicated, the Gikuyu male initiates were taught how to use weapons and the females were instructed how to work on the farm and to take care of children.

Erickson argued that at this stage, the child is in danger of developing a feeling of inadequacy and inferiority. He may despair of his tools and skills or his status among his tool partners and consider himself doomed to mediocrity. This happens when the family life has not prepared the child for school. For the traditional Gikuyu, this was not a problem. The irua trained the adolescent to work beside and with others. Instead of separating them by skill and status, irua united them in a single group—all who passed the test to adulthood. It is important to realize that for the traditional Gikuyu, agegroup and kin were the foci of a person's social life.

Erikson termed the fifth stage as an "identity versus role confusion." In this stage, childhood proper comes to an end.

The individual finds him/herself in tension between continuity and discontinuity, sameness and newness, libidinal force and society's expectation. The growing and developing youths, faced with this tangible task ahead of them are now primarily concerned with what they appear to be in the eyes of others as compared with what they feel they are, and with the question of how to connect the roles and skills cultivated earlier with the occupational prototypes of the day.

At this stage, Erikson contended that the adolescent mind is essentially in moratorium, which is a psychosocial stage between childhood and adulthood, between the morality learned by the child and the ethics to be developed by the adult. This tension may result in delinquency, over identification, aggressiveness, and diffusion of ego image. In some ways, the irua responded to this tension by mararanja, the pain of circumcision, and the ordeals during the seclusion. All these facets of the rite did help the initiates to gain an identity, but it was the rite itself that was the most important part of their new identity—it made them adults. There was no choice, no role confusion. One grew up to be one thing first, an adult—and all else is secondary. This, of course, is not true in the West.

In conclusion, the three personologists agree that the advent of puberty is accompanied by a sexual storm. An adolescent experiences conflict, which is caused by the pull between the present and non-present, reality and possibility, sexual drive and social norms.

C. Sociological Perspective

In this section we shall view the irua using the ideas set forth by Peter L. Berger and Thomas Luckman in the Social Construction of Reality. Using this insightful treatise on the sociology of knowledge, we shall conceptualize the contribution of the irua to the social construction of reality. Eventually, we shall go beyond Berger and Luckman and discuss the relationship between the irua and the adolescents' social conflict.

1. IRUA as a social construction of reality

The basic contention of Berger and Luckman is that reality is socially constructed and that a sociology of knowledge analyzes the process in which this occurs. it is evident in our study that the irua was one of the major means of the social construction of reality. The entire society participated in giving the adolescent what was regarded as authentic knowledge. As Muthoni (the daughter of Joshua, a preacher who agreed with the missionaries that female circumcision should be abolished) told Nyambura, her reason for circumcision was, "I want to be a real girl, a real woman." She wanted to be what was socially real. Berger and Luckman define the reality as a quality appertaining to phenomena that we recognize as having a being independent of our own volition. In other words, reality is that which we cannot wish away.

As we have seen several times, traditionally, there was no Gikuyu person who could be an adult without the irua. The reality of the irua was independent of an individual's decision. Until this time , every Gikuyu male must have undergone circumcision whether he liked it or not. So the irua was the conditio sine qua non of adulthood and the whole teaching of tribal law, religion, and morality. As Muthoni put it, the irua helped an individual to know "all the ways of the hills and ridges."

Thus, the irua was a means of knowing. In the words of Berger and Luckman, "Knowledge is the certainty that phenomena are real and that they possess specific characteristics. Knowledge is a social product as well as a social change.

Initiation gave the adolescent particular information, which defined for them a particular manner of conduct.

As noted, throughout the three phases of the irua, the initiates learned the language of the adult world. Comprehension of the language was and still is essential for understanding the reality of everyday life. This language, as Berger and Luckman contended, is capable of becoming the objective repository of a vast accumulation of meaning and experience, which it can then preserve in time and transmit through time to the following generation. In addition, the language that the initiates learn helps them to interpret and share their own experiences with the experiences of their fellow men.

The irua gave the initiates specific roles. They became participants and actors within the society. They shared with the adults specific goals and interlocking phases of performance. Moreover, the irua legitimized the emerging adulthood of the initiates. During the rite of bowing to the initiates, for instance, the elder not only gave his blessing, he also received blessing from the initiates. The youth were honored as mature and productive members of the community.

The irua also created what Berger and Luckman termed as a sub-universe of meaning. These authors said that Another consequence of institutional segmentation is the possibility of socially segregated subuniverses of meaning. These results from accumulation of role specialization to the point where role-specific knowledge becomes altogether esoteric as against the common stock of knowledge. Such a subuniverse of meaning may or may not be submerged for the common view ... subuniverse of meaning may be socially structured by various criteria -sex, age, occupation, religious inclination, aesthetic taste, and so on. The change of susbuniverses appearing, of course, increases steadily with progressive division of labor and economic surplus.[4]

While the irua never segregated the society in terms of black and white, upper-class and lower-class, it created a system of **age-groups in addition to the already existing societal of age-groups.** This meant that every age group acquired its own specific and unique meaning. Further, irua created a sub-universe of meaning, which was a part of the over arching symbolic universe of meaning. Every age group had esoteric knowledge, which differed from the common stock of knowledge. It had its own expressions, symbols, and rituals. This meaning was acquired after the rites of incorporation and during the age-groups' social events. It had its own language, symbols, and rituals.

It was at this time that esoteric and new knowledge, language, and rituals emerged. This was also facilitated by the events of the age-groups.

As mentioned, the Gikuyu tribe was organized by three principles—family group, clan, and age-grading. Communal work (such as building a social hall or bridge) was divided among the age-groups, which do their jobs competitively. Age-grouping, as a sub-universe of meaning, is the means of maintaining the entire symbolic universe of meaning. Likewise, this symbolic universe integrated different provinces of meaning and encompasses the institutional order in a symbo lic totality. It was also the matrix of all socially objectivated and subjectivated real meaning. The entire system of age-groupings formed one symbolic universe, which provided orders for the subjective apprehension of individual and group experiences. The experiences which belonged to various families and clans were integrated by and incorporated in the same over-arching universe of meaning—the tribe.

*In short, the **irua** facilitated the social construction of a reality in that it perpetuated the tradition of* the people, attached the individual to his primordial time and ancestral God, imparted knowledge of everyday life, and created subuniverses of meaning. Moreover, the meaning of irua was wider and deeper than Berger's and Luckman's societal construction of reality, in that one could not talk about Gikuyu society without irua. Irua was a symbol and experience through which a Gikuyu interpreted all other symbols and experiences.

2. IRUA *and the adolescent's social conflict:*

Adolescence and conflicts are inseparable. As it has been noted, the irua was the major means of ritualizing and managing adolescents' conflicts. It is evident in this discussion that conflicts are real. An adolescent's conflicts are caused by the following factors:

a. *Tension between childhood and adulthood*

On the one hand, adolescents are pulled from the world of their childhood into the demanding world of adulthood. Socially, they are expected to behave as mature persons, yet they have not been fully socialized to do so. At home they are expected to be good children, and at the same time to be responsible young men and women. Consequently, this attitude puts them in a real conflict. They do not know when they cease to be children and become full adults. This conflicts between being a child and being an adult is true of the West. The genius of the irua lay in the fact that the adults went down to the valley of childhood, leading their children out and up to the mountain top of adulthood. During the mararanja ceremonies, the adults participated in the adolescents' craziness and then led them to a disciplined life of adulthood.

b. *Independence versus dependence*

Because he is maturing, an adolescent feels a great need to be independent, but because a part of him is childlike, he remains dependent. For economic and psychological reasons the adolescent remains subordinate to his parents, yet he fights with all his might to emancipate himself. Since it is more difficult for the parents to change than the child, a teenager asserting his rights to be more grown up creates tension within the home. The irua reduced this tension in that after the initiation, young men and women were regarded as adults.

c.   *An adolescent's peer group*

Another cause of an adolescent's strife is his peer group. Although the adolescent struggles for dependence, a strong need for independence arises as he attempts to find himself and identify his role in society. Peer group plays a major part in the gratification of these needs. Thus, the peer group is an important socializing agent.

Social values and attitudes are created and reinforced by the group phenomena. Conformity demanded by his peer group makes it hard for an adolescent to be himself. The peer group is greatly responsible for the modification of behavior and for providing a forum in which the teenager sees himself, for better or worse. In most cases, there is a disagreement between the parents' attitude and the peers' expectations of an ideal social person. Thus, an adolescent hears a lot of conflicting ideas.

These problems were minimized by the irua in that the adolescents were instructed by adults during seclusion. The peer group enforced the behavior and norms, which they learned from the adult advisers. An individual clearly understood his rights and prohibitions.

d.   *Sex*

Another case of conflict is sexuality. While a typical preadolescent appears to be relatively unconfused about sexuality, with the onset of puberty and adolescence, even the most well-adjusted child will have uncertainty and become confused. A teenager feels like a learner who is driving a new car and knows very little about the power of the motor or various parts in the car. Boys are troubled by their nocturnal emissions. Girls are bothered by their emerging breast and monthly periods.

a

Part Three

CHAPTER FIVE

Irua and the Passages of Jesus

Let us think of the "passages" in terms of a safari. Suppose you have been traveling from the east to the west ever since you were born. And now you have to make an about turn and start traveling in your imagination toward the east. And you have to think and meditate on your passages starting from the most recent one. These passages may include your retirement, graduation from graduate school, undergraduate school, high school, intermediate and primary school, and the first few days in any educational institution. It may be moving to another country, province, district, location, and home or owning a farm, business, car, bicycle, cow, goat, or sheep. It may be the first appearance of gray hair, beard, secondary sex characteristics, and so on. Go as far as you can. As you meditate on each of these passages, ask yourself, *What are the major motifs in all my passages?* Write all these motifs on a paper. Then have a flash-back on what you have read about the irua. Jot down all the motifs that you can remember. Then think about the motifs of Jesus of Nazareth, which are recorded in the New Testament. After this, conceptualize the motifs in the irua and your pilgrimage with those in Jesus.

My list includes the following motifs: separation, transition, incorporation, instruction, feeding, antistructure (mararanja), structure, division of labor, the Tree of God, the Great Mother, the Great Father, community, individuality, sex, submissiveness, silence, humiliation, pain, precariousness, identity, exaltation, and joy. In this chapter we shall discuss the passages of Jesus, as delineated by the community of faith, in the light of the irua motifs.

To have a meaningful discussion of the passages of Jesus, we must respond to two questions which are posed by the New Testament scholars. Do we have a historical account of the life of Jesus Christ? Are the Gospels biographies of Jesus?

The majority of the New Testament theologians question the historicity of the Gospel. R. Bultmann asserts, thatthe history of Jesus in the sense of that which may be learned from historical research, is no more than a walk through a museum of antiquities. For Bultmann, a search for the historical Jesus is historically impossible and theologically illegitimate. Martin Dibelius, in his book, *Jesus*, contends that what is asserted by faith cannot be demonstrated at every corner. What we have, according to Dibelius, is a Christ of faith.t. Some scholars, like William Barclay, would even argue that, the Jesus of history and Christ of faith have no necessary connection. Neo-orthodox theologians, like Donald Baillie, Karl Barth, and Emil Brunner says, "faith presupposes as a matter of course, a priori, that the Jesus of history is not the same as the Christ of 'faith. In faith we are not concerned with the Jesus of history as historical science sees him, but with the Jesus Christ of personal testimony, who is the real Christ.

These scholars agree that the Jesus of history (that which is merely historical, that which is simply past, that which has no particular relevance to my life, that which makes no special demand on me) and the Christ Geshchichte (that with which I am still faced, that which still demands a response and decision from me, that which I do not merely know, but on which I must act) are not the same. It then applies that we do not have biographies of Jesus—as William Barclay writes, "Biography we do not have; portrait we certainly possess." Thus, what we have is the early ecclesial community's characterization and portrait of Christ.

It is from this understanding that we shall conceptualize the motifs in Jesus' passages with the irua motifs. By the phrase "motifs in Jesus' passages," I mean the central and salient themes in the ecclesial community of the early centuries, which are ascribed to Jesus by the New Testament writers. By "irua motifs" I mean central and salient themes in the Gikuyu community's life cycle, which were ritualized by the irua. It is hoped that this conceptualization will lead us to an African Christological model. The scope of this work does not allow us to discuss fully the deity of Christ. The passages of Jesus that will be discussed include birth, naming, circumcision, puberty rites, liminality, ministry, death, and resurrection.

A. *The Birth of Jesus and the Irua Motifs*

Like the irua and the birth of the Gikuyu child, the birth rites of Jesus included community, joy, thanksgiving, and exaltation. Luke writes that after the birth of Jesus, "suddenly there was with the angels a multitude of the heavenly hosts praising God saying, 'Glory to God in the highest and on earth peace among men with whom he is well pleased'" (2:13-14). Here Luke indicates that Jesus was born to a community and for the community. This is similar to what we have seen in the birth of a Gikuyu child. The midwife and her team reported to the husband, "We have seen men," not man or "We have seen women," not woman. While birth brought one to the world of community, the irua made one an active member of that community. As with the Gikuyu initiation, the birth of Jesus was attended by a gathering, who made a shout of joy. The shepherds were joyful and praised God for what they had seen, and for the fact that the Great Shepherd had become human. The Wise Men "rejoiced exceedingly with great joy," because the eternal logos who pre-existed with God had become a human child, better still, a human community. As a thanksgiving to God, they presented to the child gold, frankincense, and myrrh. As we have seen, the new born babies and the initiates were given presents. The relatives and friends gave the initiates presents to express their appreciation for the new born.

B. The Naming and Circumcision of Jesus and Irua Motifs

Unlike the naming of a Gikuyu child, which was connected with birth, the naming of Jesus was connected with circumcision. In contrast, the Gikuyu circumcision was a puberty rite; the Jewish circumcision was an infantile rite. Both rites symbolize newness and becoming a part of a community. Like the Gikuyu names, the name of Jesus has a meaning. It means a savior who will deliver his people from their sins (Matthew 2:21).

After the naming and circumcision, Jesus was presented in the temple. Here he met Simeon and Anna, representatives of the community who gave their prophetic insight concerning the child and his mission. For Simeon, Jesus was the savior, the light, and judge of the oikumene—all the inhabited world. For Anna, Jesus was the object of worship, the redeemer of Jerusalem, the city of God. This rich story includes three mythological motifs, which will be discussed in part four. These are the Tree of God (Jerusalem), the Great Father (Simeon) and the Great Mother (Anna). The book of Revelation, which is so rich in symbolism, describes Jerusalem as the Tree of God in which there are twelve kinds of fruits—yielding its fruit each month, and the leaves of the tree were for the healing of the nations. So Jerusalem is to the Jews what the Mukuyu is to the Gikuyu. As we shall see later, the Mukuyu is more than a tree, it is a mythological motif. Simeon and Anna are analogous to the Great Father and Great Mother who dwell in the nyumba and the Thingira. As we shall see later, Nyumba and Thingira are not necessarily buildings. Like the Gikuyu initiates, Jesus was presented to the Tree of God, the Great Mother, and Great Father. When Jesus was twelve years of age, he had to undergo a puberty rite in the Great City—Jerusalem.

C. Jesus' Visit to the Temple and Irua Motifs

Thanks to Luke, the portrait of Jesus is far from that of a phantom. Unlike the docetic boy, Jesus of the Apocryphal Gospel of Thomas who taught the rabbis, Jesus went to the temple to worship and to learn Jewish customs. Like Gikuyu boys, Jesus went to the Great Tree (Mukuyu), the symbol of the origin and the totality of ontology of the Israelites. The motifs that are included in this rite are precariousness, pain, instruction, and joy.

It is evident in our discussion that the irua externalized and ritualized the psychological dynamics of the adolescents. An adolescent feels confused because of his parent's demands and the demand of his peers and his community. He does not want to be taken care of as a child because he is not a child; yet, he is not mature enough and does not have sufficient resources to care for himself/herself. Jesus wanted freedom to be away from his parents (which he was granted) and to be in his Father's House. As any other boy, he did not want his parents to interfere with his religious freedom. This is why he asked them, "How is it that you sought me? Don't you know I have to be in my Father's house?" Yet, he was not mature enough to join the caravan at the right time. Jesus was not different from our youngsters who are good at going out to have a good time with their peer group, yet are unable to come at the right time for dinner. My point is that Jesus, as any healthy adolescent, experienced the pull between home and society.

The incident was painful to the parents and to Jesus himself. The parents were angry to discover "after a day's journey" that Jesus was not with them. They had to go back and did not find Jesus until the third day. When they saw him, Mary expressed her real parental anger, "Son, why have you treated us so?" Jesus had to rationalize as any other clever boy, "Did you not know that I must be in my Father's house?" It was also painful for Jesus to learn that he had forced his parents to walk back "a day's journey." This painful moment was a time for great learning. The parents of Jesus found him "sitting among the teachers, listening to them and asking questions." As the Gikuyu initiates, he got instruction from the senior advisor about his roots and religion.

Jesus, like the Gikuyu initiates, experienced the joy of becoming. He had a joyous feeling for "all who heard him were amazed at his understanding and his answers." By being listened to, he became more aware of the fact that he was growing as an independent individual and that he has come from God and has to be always in the Father's house. He ascertained that he was loved by "God and man," and as a Gikuyu initiate, he became more aware of his role in society. The visit to Jerusalem enhanced his self-identity as a Messiah who was also a Suffering Servant.

D. *The Liminality of Jesus and the Irua Motifs*

As it was with the Africans and other people, Jesus' passages were marked with liminal experiences. At his conception, his mother and Joseph were debased for having a pregnancy without an earthly father. During birth, Jesus and his parents were debased by being born in a manger because there was no place for him in the inn. The crib of the Lord of the universe was a manger. Even though he was the Lord of cosmos, and that it was in him that all things hold together, even though he was God, he emptied himself. He became a human being taking a form of a slave and totally submitted himself to God's will. The Lord of all creation humbled "Himself and became obedient to death, even the death on the cross." Philippians 2:8 (RSV) As a suffering servant, "he was despised and rejected by men, a man of sorrow and acquainted with grief. He was wounded for our transgression; upon him was the chastisement that made us whole and with his stripes we are healed."Isaiah 53:3-5(RSV)

Like Ndembu, chief-elect, Jesus was denied of what he possessed and what he was to become. But unlike the former, the latter was wounded for our transgression. He suffered that we might be made whole. Unlike the African initiate, Jesus was humiliated to death, even the death on the cross. The greater the suffering, however, the greater was his glorification. After death, he rose with a spiritual, everlasting, and non-aging body. And as Paul writes, "God has highly exalted him and bestowed on him a name that is above every name, that at the name of Jesus every knee should bow, in the heaven and on earth and under the earth and that every tongue confess that Jesus is Lord, to the glory of God the Father."Philippian 2:9-11

For those of us who are bearers of Christ, marginalization and glorification are recurring experiences in our earthly pilgrimage. Most of, if not all, the Saints and architects of Christian faith and the true prophets underwent intensive suffering. Their suffering was either psychological or physical or both. Paul speaks for us, "We are afflicted in every way, but not crushed; perplexed, but not driven to despair; persecuted but not forsaken; struck down but not destroyed, always carrying in the body the death of Jesus, so that the life of Jesus may be manifested in our bodies." As the bearers of the Suffering Servant we are despised, ridiculed, gossiped about, and reviled. Sometimes we feel alienated from the people of our own kind, family, neighbors, and from our tool-partners. At the heat of the desert, we may feel as though the Deity has hid his countenance from us. Jesus showed his feeling on the cross when he cried, "My God, My God! Why hast thou forsaken me?"

Yet, when we pass through limbo successfully, we become more refined and useful to God and the human family. We become a blessing. Hence, Jesus exhorts, "Blessed are you when men will revile you and persecute you and utter all kinds of evil against you falsely on my account. Rejoice and be glad, for your reward is great in heaven." Matthew 5:11-12 Thus the bearers of the truth experience pain and joy, humiliation and exaltation. They possess both the death and life of Christ in their bodies.

Gikuyu initiates were vested with white robes after the ordeal of their marginal entity. The white robes symbolized the newness of life. Like the Gikuyu initiates, at the end of all things, Christian victors will be clothed with white robes. But different from the Gikuyu initiates, Christian victors will be clothed with spiritual white robes, which will remain stainless forever. They will reign with Christ forever. The dwelling of God (Shekinah) will be with them and they will be totally free from any form of tribulation.

In this chapter, an attempt has been made to show that the motifs that are inherent in the African rites of passage are also found in the passages of Christ. It is very difficult to understand the reason why there are parallel motifs between Jesus' life and the Gikuyu culture. It could be due to cultural contact, common human needs, or the objective psyche. The comparison of the Gikuyu with the Hebrews indicates that the two people had similar myths. Like Abraham, Gikuyu was promised the inheritance of the land, becoming a people through a divine providence. Yahweh miraculously provided Abraham and Sarah with a son who later became the father of the nation. In the same way Ngai provided Gikuyu and Mumbi with nine sons who became the fathers of a tribe. The two people use circumcision as the mark of the covenant and as a means of initiating an individual into the community. Sacrifices have a significant place in both religions. In addition, the two people have holy mountains. Thus it is most probable that the similarity between the motifs in the life of Jesus and the life of the Gikuyu is due to the fact that the Israelites and the Gikuyu have similar religious and social structures.

Further, the two people, being human societies, possess a psychic unity that could affect the occurrence of similar rites, myths and symbols. Moreover, as we have mentioned and will further discuss in the following chapters, the archetypal motifs, which are intrinsic in the Gikuyu people are also inherent in other human families. In the following chapters, we shall identify and discuss the archetypal motifs of human personality.

a

Part Four

THE ARCHETYPAL MOTIFS
OF HUMAN PERSONALITY

By the term archetype motif, we mean elements, subjects, themes and forms which move from the unconscious to the conscious and the back to unconscious. While each of the archetypal motif is always in the psyche, occasionally, it gains supremacy over other archetypal motifs and then submerges in order to give way to the others. There is a swirling movement in both an individual;s and community's life cycle.Some of them are contrasting. The contrasting archetypal motifs includes communality and individuality to which we now turn.

CHAPTER SIX

Communality and Individuality

It is axiomatic in our discussion that the Gikuyu community expected an individual to balance between communality and individuality. The communality aspect of personality was ritualized from birth to death. We noted that after birth, the midwife and her assistants reported the sex of the infant in plural form. For instance, if the first-born was a male, they reported to the father, "We have seen men and it is your father." This was an indication that the child was born as and to the community. We have also noted that the community participated in all the rites of passage of an individual.

In addition, the individual aspect of personality was recognized throughout the life cycle. Even at birth, the community realized that one was born as a separate and unique being. The report from the midwife to the father showed that, while the baby boy was "men" he was also "your father," meaning that he would be called after the fathers' father. In most cases, as the child grew and started demonstrating unique traits, he was given a nickname.

The nicknaming was a gesture showing that although the child was named after someone else, he was a unique character. During the rite of second birth, while the community was involved, the boy or a girl was taken back to the mother's womb alone. This ritual symbolized the fact that the person was becoming a separate individual.

This individual aspect of personality was also evident during the actual day of operation whereby one had one's own share of being "bitten by the knife." One felt pain alone. It is through this individual experience, I believe, that the Gikuyu coined a proverb: "Pain cannot be felt by one for the other." The community was aware of the fact that each person, being different from all other persons, has his own peculiar cross which he has to bear. He may also bring with him to the world a unique contribution.

A. Communality

The Gikuyu people expected a person to be born as a community to contribute to and draw from a mutual and inclusive community. This community included those yet to be born, the living, and the dead.

1. A Mutual Community

The mutual aspect of community was expressed by a proverb: "A small red snuff-box is a reciprocity" (Kanya gatune mwamukaniro). The proverb refers to the Gikuyu custom of giving a pinch of snuff to friends when you meet. This demonstrates the fact that what one has, belongs to him and his friends. The proverb also denotes that a healthy social life was that which was a give-and-take process.

An individual was expected to contribute to his needs and those of the community. An unhealthy person was one who lived for himself. The rich person who did not receive from others was also regarded as communally unhealthy. A healthy rich person was one who could borrow a needle from his neighbor. And a healthy poor person was the one who could lend a needle to the rich. No matter how rich or poor a person was, he was expected to reciprocate.

2. An Inclusive Community

The Gikuyu community was inclusive. That is, one belonged to all in the village, and all in the village belonged to him. That is, one was a son or a daughter of all, a father or mother of all, and a grandfather or grandmother of all. A wide range of relatives, neighbors, and villagers shared the responsibility for the education and discipline of children and youths. The aged, deformed, insane, and orphans were cared for by all. The irua was the basis of this wider inclusive community. Without it there would be only kinship and the community would stop with ties of blood. The irua on the other hand created a community across kin ties. It took all of the initiates and placed them in their community as age-mates above their particular and differing kin ties.

The Gikuyu community never segregated someone because he was either white or black, tall or short, fat or thin, beautiful or ugly. However, if she was too white she could be nicknamed "white" (mweru), if too black he could be called "black" (muiru), and so on. But he or she was accepted fully as a member of the society. Interestingly, although Christian priesthood was superficially denominationalized, it was profoundly seen as a function in the community. The priest in a particular locality belonged to all the people in that area, whether they were Christians, non-Christians, or Muslims.

3. A Community of Both the Living and Dead

The Gikuyu community was a community of both the living and the dead. While they never worshipped the ancestors, the Gikuyu, like other African people, communicated with their "living-dead." An individual was, therefore, made aware of the fact that he was influenced by both the present community and his ancestors.

The influence of the ancestors has been identified by C.J. Jung. According to Jung, the psyche includes the conscious and the unconscious. The unconscious comprises the subjective level, which he termed the personal unconscious. This realm consists of all those contents that became unconscious because consciousness was withdrawn from them. The personal unconscious is the product of an individual's subjective experience.

This is that part of a person that is influenced by the community in which he lives in his life-time.

The other realm is on the objective level, which Jung termed "the collective unconscious." Later in his work, he referred to this realm as "the objective psyche." Jung asserted that this supra-individual psychic activity is the ancestral heritage of a personality. It comprises mythological motifs and archetypes. These archetypes are psychic imprints, inborn patterns of experience. While the content of the archetypes is filled by the life of an individual, the form is inherited and pre-existent.

Viewed from the Jungian perspective, communication with the ancestors is a communication between the conscious and the objective psyche. Furthermore, the African belief on communication with the ancestors,[i] and the Christian doctrine of the communication of the saints encourages us to be aware of and listen to the part of us which is ancestral—the pre-existent self.

However, some Gikuyu, as it is also with other African people, tend to give undue power to the words of the departed. Some can even be bothered by what they think (or are deceived by others into thinking) the dying relative said about them. They fear a curse. For instance, my paternal grandfather's family does not eat the liver because, according to the family's myth, one of the family warriors went to the Masai land to raid cattle. This warrior captured a large number of cattle. On his way home, he remembered his liver, which he had forgotten in Masai Land. When he went back to fetch it, he was killed by a Masai warrior. Before he died, it was thought he said, "All the men in the family shall not eat the liver."

For a Christian, this curse is groundless and powerless. My father destroyed the curse by giving us the liver when we were children. We have never suffered any misfortune because of eating the liver. This type of groundless and conditioning curses can be removed by Christ who is above and transforms culture.

However, it is healthy to accept the fact that in our souls dwells the archetypes of the father, mother, grandfather, grandmother, and of our distant ancestors. These archetypes influence our behavior and our perception and interpretation of reality.

Thus, man not only lives in a community, but is intrinsically communal. Urban T. Holmes, in his Ministry and Imagination[1] recognized the communality of man. He contended that "man is by nature communal." He is a city creature and a product of his environment. Holmes rightly maintains that "all life is a shared existence." He regards the Christian ministry as what a Church does to make Christ a living reality in the community. For Holmes, the goal of ministry is "the perfected social reality." One could argue that one of the objectives of religion is to help an individual, who is regarded as one of the organs in the body. He has a special contribution to make in order that the whole body may be edified. In addition, he has to live in the body so that he may draw the flow of life from the body, that he may grow as a faithful, hopeful, and loving individual.

4. Communality and Counseling

In counseling, we need to realize that our client is a part of, and is affected by, all the groups to which he is a member. He is first of all a member of what Charles Horton Cooley termed a "primary group." This group includes the family and the clique. It is characterized by intimacy, face-to-face interaction, mutual identification, and "we feeling." The primary group is based on a shared point of view. The members of the primary group agree on many aspects of life. An individual shares with his primary group his sadness and joy, his innermost feelings, and most personal experiences.

Bearing this in mind, we need to have a good knowledge of the characteristics of the primary group, family in particular, to which our client is a part. We should ask the following questions: *What are the blessings and curses of the family? What is regarded as the most important and least important? Does the family have an oversupply of a particular quality of life or gift? What is the weakest aspect of the family? What are norms and values of the family? How does the family hinder the counseling process? Is there a discrepancy between the family's ideal and the individual's potentials?* If it is marriage counseling, we need to watch out whether there is conflict of values in the couple's families of origin. For instance, the husband's family of origin may lay much emphasis on work, while the wife's family of origin may put stress on having a "good time." The husband may regard the whole of life as work. He may not know what it is to have leisure time. The wife, on the other hand, may expect the whole of life to be "a good time" and regard work as a bondage and regard her husband a slave to work. On the other hand, the husband may regard his wife's "good time" as laziness. In this case, the counselor should ask himself: *How can I facilitate these partners so that they may complement each other?* Needless to say, we need to realize that if the client's problem arises from conflict in the primary group, the hurt is deeper than it would be if it would be in a secondary group. In this case, we need to seek to reconcile this person with his group and guide him to act constructively. It should be realized that the members of the family group are a part of the individual archetypes. For this reason, a constant fight with it means a constant conflict within one's soul.

Thus, the primary group is essential to us in that we have face-to-face interaction. In this relationship, we share the reality of everyday life. We become fully real. And as Berger and Luckman put it, "My and his 'here and now' continuously impinge on each other as long as the face-to-face situation continues."[2] Here, I would go further than these authors. In the face-to-face relationship with our family group we share our past—the old bad days and the old good days—our present and our future. We re-live our "child" and associate with our parents—whether they are living or dead—and sharpen our future goals. The family group creates a feeling of wholeness. For these reasons, successful counseling is that which reconciles an individual with his family groups.

Moreover, it should be born in mind that an individual belongs to a reference group that possesses a standard against which he assesses himself. This provides a measurement of how an individual is performing. While these groups can lead to personal development, it can also arouse a feeling of jealousy and inadequacy. This group can throw a person into what sociologists term *relative deprivation*. That is, one feels that he is worse than his tool partners. Although a feeling of deprivation may make a person protest against his inferior self and challenge him to strive for higher things and, therefore, improve himself and his environments, one should bear in mind that he is an individual with his own peculiar limitations and strengths.

In addition, we should be aware of the fact that human personality is affected by the secondary groups. These groups, unlike primary groups, are impersonal, mechanical, and have superficial and casual relations. These groups are more concerned with work than intimacy. The factory group is one of the best examples. The member of this group is controlled by both the management and machine. The concern of the owner of the factory is production, while the worker is interested in earning a living. The worker has no connection with the production. He also has only a superficial relationship with other workers. The individual lives in alienation. He is alienated from his product and from the community in which he spends eight hours a day.

How to improve human conditions in places of work is an issue that should be considered by both the employer and the workers. While the employer has to see to it that the work is done, he should appreciate the workers as human beings and reward them for the work that they have done. He should employ positive, rather than negative, reinforcement.

It could also be rewarding if the worker could work for the sake of work itself, rather than just working only for the sake of money. We should view work as an integral part of life, rather than a punishment. Interestingly, the

Bible delineates the creation of man as a part of God's work. God was the first worker. Further, it indicates that man was created in order to work. It says, "The Lord God took the man and put him in the garden of Eden to till it and keep it" (Genesis 2:15).

Work preceded the fall. So it is not a result of sin, but a part of God's creation. So, rather than see work as a torture, we should love it and be proud of it.

It could be psychologically and spiritually healthy if we do not expect to enjoy the same intimacy in the work-group (secondary group) as we enjoy in the family group. If we expect this type of love, we are expecting to achieve something that is impossible. And this will only widen the gap between our ideal and reality.

However, whether we are with the primary group, secondary group, or reference group we should be aware of the fact that we are both communal and individual. As individuals we are different from one another. Each one of us has a different perception and interception and interpretation of reality and he was created in order to make a special contribution to the human family.

B. Individuality

Individuality in the Gikuyu Community

The Gikuyu community encouraged and challenged one to be an individual. There are several proverbs and expressions that clarify this point. To mention just a few, the Gikuyu says, "Ndiakagwo ta ya wakini"—"One does not construct his family as that of his age-group brother." This proverb implies that, although during the initiation the individuals receive the same instruction, one is expected to have his own philosophy and to fashion his family differently. The husband was advised to treat his wife differently, because she was an individual. The wife was also instructed not to anticipate her husband to be like the husband of her friend. Although the couple was expected to impart the whole gamut of the tribe's culture, values and norms to their children they were required to bring them up as individuals.

Another proverb that is used for rebuking a person who fears to be himself says "Mwigerekanio wariire ciura matina"— "Imitation ate the frog's buttocks." According to the Gikuyu myths, the frogs once had big buttocks, which they lost because of their bad habit of mimicking. This proverb was used for the people who over-identified themselves with the others. The Gikuyu believed that those who aped others lost their buttocks. That is, they lost their unique and essential self, they had nothing of their own to contribute to the community. Thus, an individual was expected to be himself and to give his very self, and not another person, to the society.

Individuality and Biology and Psychology

Biology and psychology confirm the fact that we are individuals. Each person has a different appearance. He walks and talks differently, He views and interprets the environment differently. Consequently he is molded differently by the environment.

Our individuality is in-born. It starts from our mother's womb when the egg cell and sperm cell unite. The two consist of forty-six chromosomes, half of which are supplied by the father through the chromosomes of the sperm, while the other half are acquired from the mother by the chromosomes of the ovum. Each of these chromosomes consist of several hundred of genes. These genes are responsible for transmission of traits of height and the color of the skin, hair, and eyes. Our variation is due to the fact that during the union of the egg cell and the sperm, the pairing of two sets of chromosomes from the two parents both have a diverse heredity background of their own. This results in the variables is seen in our faces and bodies. And for this reason, no two individuals ever chance to be identical.

Since we are biologically different, we react differently to both our internal and external environment. Consequently, the society in which we live reacts toward us differently. Thinking of the environment as a river, one could contend that no two individuals ever cross the same river, and no two individuals ever draw the same water from the same river. Since we have different points of view, different perception and different interpretations of experience, we tend to draw, attract, and allow a different quality of dimension of the flow of life. As a result, the environment plants in our personalities varied seeds, and we bear different fruits. Thus both we and our environment contribute to our individuality.

The person-centered personality theory of Carl Rogers recognizes and emphasizes the individuality of personality more than any other theory. Rogers, influenced by Kierkegaard, regards the goal and purpose of human life as being "that self which one truly is." Rogers believes that a healthy person is one who can listen to, accept, and be himself. This person who has accepted himself, will also be in a position of listening and allowing his neighbor to be himself. Rogers asserted that when a person listens to his "I-ness" and his neighbors' "I-ness" he becomes creatively realistic and realistically creative.

Listening to and becoming ourselves is one of the hardest tasks. This is difficult not only for African people, but also Western people. This point can be illustrated with an experience I had with a patient when I was doing clinical pastoral education at Milledgeville State Hospital in Georgia. One day, I received a call from the head nurse asking me to talk to a patient who had refused to talk to the nurses and doctors and to take her medicine. I went hurriedly to the ward where I was given the room. The patient, who was a thirty-two-year-old alcoholic, white woman was brought to me. We sat together and had a dialogue, which went as follows:

Githiga: "How are things with you?"

Patient: "They're all talking behind my back."

Githiga: "Talking about you?"

Patient: "All the doctors, nurses, and patients are slandering me."

Githiga: "Are they talking about you?"

Patient: "Yes."

Githiga: "What are they saying?"

Patient: "I saw them talking, but I didn't know what they were saying."

Githiga: "So you are not sure whether they were talking about you?"

Patient: "I am not sure."

Githiga: "What do you say about yourself?"

Patient: Pointing at herself: "Me, I don't know, me."

Githiga: "So you don't know yourself?"

Patient: "I was born and brought up by a very domineering mother, who always told me what to do. She never allowed me to initiate anything and so from her I learned not to listen to myself. This is why I am bothered by what other people think and talk about me."

Githiga: "And possibly you are bothered by what you think they are thinking about you rather than what they are actually thinking about you."

To make a long story short, this woman had a real problem in listening to herself and becoming herself. She was a slave of what other people said about her. Being sick of course, the voice of the group was exaggerated. But even those of us who are not as sick tend to allow the "we-ness" to suppress our "I-ness." In African society, where the accent is put on communality, we tend to ignore our unique self through which we can discover a new truth and reality, which could help us to affect change and development.

In conclusion, we should learn how to balance between the self and collective. We should ask ourselves the following questions: *Am I losing my individuality in conventionality? Am I allowing my "I-ness" to be suppressed by the "we-ness"? Do I have courage to be? Do I appreciate and take the freedom of being which is granted to me by the community? Do I value the important social norms of my community? Do I have an extreme self-love, which expects the whole world to revolve around me in order to satisfy me?*

Am I only living for myself?

An individual must be in the community in order to be himself so that he may contribute to the community. Man was created as both "I" and "We." As the book of Genesis tells us, "For God created man in His own image...male and female he created them." As this verse indicates, the human person is individual, communal, and sexual.

a

CHAPTER SEVEN

Initiation and Human Sexuality

A. *What is Sexuality?*

The word sexuality will be used in a wider sense to denote vital spiritual energy. It will also refer to the drive, which makes human persons long for bodily and emotional intimacy. This vital spiritual energy is demonstrated by hand-shaking, hugging, teasing, and smiling. This energy gives us a loving, warm, and cordial feeling towards one another. This vital spiritual energy, which emanates from God, entices us to God and helps us cling to one another. This energy makes religious love more lively and attractive.

The word "sex" will refer to our maleness and femaleness, that which distinguishes masculine gender from feminine gender. It will also refer to both primary and secondary sexual organs. The word "coitus," "sexual intercourse," "an affair" will be used for full sexual intercourse.

As indicated, sex was given a supreme position during the initiation. It was highly praised and exalted. Most of the songs that were sung at this occasion were about sexual organs and sexual behavior. During this time, sex language was learned. Children and the initiates acquired most of the information about reproductive systems and sexual morality. In addition, children had the freedom of observing the genitals during the actual day of circumcision.

Furthermore, during the seclusion period, sex education was imparted to the youths. Young women learned about menstruation and how to handle the boys. Young men were taught how to care for and respect women and how to relate to them as partners rather than sexual objects. Moreover, the study has shown that the traditional Gikuyu community used sexual intercourse to console the bereaved and the lonely. We have also found that most of the rites commenced and were concluded with a symbolic sexual act. This demonstrates the fact that sex was used as a sacrament.

B. Sex Education in African Tradition and Missionary Schools

Initiation, which was the African traditional school, offered sex education in both theory and practice. This school was replaced with the missionary schools, which appeared to have negative attitudes toward human sexuality. By waging war against initiation and segregating boys from girls in the schools and men from women in the churches, it became apparent to the Africans that

Christianity was opposed to all matters pertaining to sexual behavior. Until very recently, the overseas churches, from where the missionaries came, had not addressed this subject. It was as recent as 1965 that the British Council of Churches elected the commission to study "sex and morality." This commission found that "the matter is not so simple." It reported that "the thinking of our group has been so far removed from this (simplicity) as to challenge the idea that there is a Christian position at all." Since the missionaries did not have any "position at all,"[2] they could not give any guidance to their young churches about human sexuality.

In the Roman Catholic scene, it was in the fall of 1972 that the Board of Directors of the Catholic Theological Society of America commissioned a committee to do a study on human sexuality in the hope of "providing some helpful and illuminating guidelines in the present confusion." This committee found that the Catholic attitude toward human sexuality was both complex and contradictory.[3]

The liquidation of the traditional school and the placing of it with schools that transmitted contradicting theories about sexuality has led to subversive sexual behavior in East Africa.

C. Sex and Morality in Kenya

Presently in Kenya, sex is being used by men and women as a means of mutual exploitation. Boys and girls have been abused and demoralized by adults. Boys are being used as sex objects by the rich "sugar mummies." The white old women tourists have been seen at the

Kenya Coast walking hand in hand with boys. These women entice the boys with money and make them their playmates. By being supplied with a large sum of money, the boys abandon their schooling to join with their older sexual partners. When these boys are left by their "sugar mummies," they become delinquents.

And, finally, they become robbers.

School girls are the most victimized group in our soci ety. They are being abused by their age mates, their teachers, wealthy tycoons, the working class, and tourists. Consequently, pregnancy among school girls has become a frequent occurrence. Too many girls are dropping out of school to give birth. Most of them never come back to school after delivering. They end up being barmaids or prostitutes. While men abuse school girls and of course mature women, they are, in turn, being exploited by both the prostitutes and the working women. For instance, a woman who is an assistant sales manager earning a middle class salary was reported to have boasted she expects Kshs 500 (a normal monthly wage of a person of lower class) each time she sleeps with a man. She bragged, "The married ones are the best. They want a variety and no commitment… so they look for a discreet, employed single girl like me who will take the money and keep her mouth shut." Here one can note that this woman not only drains the men's wallets, but also can disrupt marriages. For this woman, as it is with others, sex is a commodity that can be sold over and over again. For some of the women in our society, sex has become merchandise. This fact is well demonstrated by a woman writer who argued that "some people sell cooking fat, others sell coffee beans for profit. Do these have any right to tell a woman not to sell herself?"[4]

As noted, the traditional school trained women in such a way that they could not sell themselves.In contemporary Africa, female are selling themselves to the tourists.. Half a million tourists flock into Kenya every year. While some of them come to enjoy the game parks and fine beaches, others, notably Germans, choose Kenya primarily because of cheap and willing sexual partners. One German tourist was reported to have said that he changes girlfriends like his pants. This man believes that he is not the exception, because "in Germany, the word has spread around that Kenya is almost as good for a sex-holiday as Bangkok." Most of the victims are teenage girls or young women who have either abandoned schooling, are jobless, or earn minimal salaries in Mombasa and other tourist zones. On the one hand, these women get money, on the other hand they feel demoralized and dehumanized. According to one of the victims, "They (the tourists) think they are the greatest and we are half-animals."

As noted, one of the causes of sexual maladjustment in a changing society is the fact that the missionary schools and churches did not provide a positive sex education. Worse still, even when the leadership of these schools and Churches was taken by the Africans, the African teachers and pastors were dominated by what President Kenneth Kaunda of Zambia terms as a "black version of Seventeenth Century English Puritans." The African Puritanism went far beyond the missionary one. All sex and social activities (like dancing) were regarded as the sin of sins. A Christian priest was partly seen as a symbol of an asexualized deity. For this reason, the parishioners were, and still are, free to discuss with the priest all other problems except sexual problems. Christian youth came to regard sex as a "forbidden fruit," which Adam and Eve ate and what consequently brought death to humankind. The Church's and the school's attitude posed a discrepancy between the seemingly asexualized society and the actual sexual energy which was intrinsic in every healthy individual. As we shall see later, this distance between the actuality and ideality of human sexuality was one of the causes of mass hysteria in girls' boarding schools. As we have seen in the preceding pages, the modern school has not succeeded in preparing youth for the present society, which is not only experiencing the flocking in of tourists, but also experiencing an explosion of knowledge.

D. Initiation and Positive Teaching About Human Sexuality

It is evident in our study that the irua gave a positive teaching about human sexuality. Children, youth and adults were made aware of the fact that they were essentially and fundamentally sexual beings. This truth can be affirmed both theologically and psychologically.

It is clear in the creation story that God created humans as male and female. As the narrator stated, "So God created man in his own image, in the image of God he created him; male and female he created them" (Genesis 1:27). As this verse indicates, there is a close relationship between the image of God and human sexuality. Hence eros is God- given. Indeed, it is one of the attributes of

God. Since there is nothing in God which is not giving and nothing good in humankind which is not given by God, eros is one of the most precious gifts that God has given to human beings.

As Hans Kung rightly contended, eros (love as desire) and agape (love that gives) are inseparable. He asked, "Can we say, therefore, not eros, but agape? Could not someone desire another person and yet be able at the same time to give himself? And on the other hand, is not a person who gives himself also permitted to desire the other? Does not the God of the Old Testament desire his people of Israel passionately, with "jealousy," as the prophets say, like a man who loves his faithless wife? Is not God's covenant with his people thus represented in symbols of eros as marriage and the people's desertion as adultery? Was not the Song of Songs a collection of sensual love songs admitted in the Old Testament Canon? And does not God's love in the New Testament have very human features—the love of a father who wants his prodigal son back?"[5] As Kung indicated, true love, which is portrayed by the scriptures, does not exclude eros. It is eros that makes agape attractive and fills us with vitality, emotion, affection, warmth, intimacy, tenderness, and cordiality.

With this understanding, religious people should not regard human sexuality as a "forbidden fruit," but should accept joyfully and gratefully that they are sexual beings. Sexuality is "willed by God, created as something good, about which human beings need not be embarrassed or ashamed in any way."[6]

1. Psychology and Irua Philosophy

Psychology agrees with irua philosophy that we are sexual beings. Freud, the father of psychoanalysis, argued, "The new-born infant brings sexuality with it into the world, certain sexual sensations attend to its development while at the breast and during early childhood, only very few children would seem to escape some kind of sexual experiences before puberty."[7] According to Freud, we are born and develop as sexual persons. Like a traditional Gikuyu community, he was aware of the fact that during puberty, the genitals acquire supremacy among all the zones and sources of pleasure.[8] For Freud, sexuality was not only an instinct, rather all instincts were basically sexual.[9]

Furthermore, he regarded sexual maladjustment as one of the causes of neurosis. This maladjustment results from the mismanagement of the conflicts, which are related to psychosexual development. In the first stage, the oral phase, the erogenous zone is in the mouth, the primary activities are receiving and taking, and the important area of conflict is feeding. This stage is followed by the anal phase, whereby the erogenous zone is the anus. The primary activities are giving and withholding, preservation and destruction; toilet training is the important area of conflict. This continues until the third stage, which is phallic. During the phallic stage, the erogenous zone is the genitals. The boy idealizes, treasures, and attaches pride to his penis. This is the stage of the famous Oedipus complex, whereby the child competes with the same-sexed parent. If the boy is coerced he may develop castration anxiety. Following the phallic phase is latency. In this stage the sexual instinct is dormant. The child learns skills that are not directly related to sexuality. The latency stage is characterized by mature sexuality that combines all that is learned in the pre-genital stages. Freud asserted that at this stage, an individual relies primarily upon intercourse and orgasm. A person who reaches this stage successively is fully able to love and work.

When the conflict encountered at each of these stages is minimal in intensity, the stage is successfully passed over. But if the parent intensifies the conflict by depriving or by being too inconsistent, the growth is arrested. This arresting is called fixation. it signifies that the activities of the psychosexual stage involved during the arresting will remain important to the person even after he has achieved puberty. Worse still, this can be a source of the occurrence of massive defensiveness aimed at avoiding anxiety through avoiding conflicts. Aware of the conflicts related to psychosexual development, Freud felt strongly that children should be told the truth about sex from the earliest time possible. A traditional Gikuyu child learned about sex at a very early stage.

2. Telling Children the Truth About Human Sexuality

We have noted that all pre-circumcision dances were about sex. During this time, children not only learned the names of all parts of sexual organs, they learned sexual behavior as well. When we were children, we used to enjoy jokes and mutual confrontation between men and women. We could hear a woman shouting to a man: "Look at him. He is impotent! He cannot erect!" These types of expressions gave us an opportunity to know something about sex and sexual behavior.

Modern sex researchers have often compared the development of sexual behavior with the learning of a language. Human beings can learn to respond to a great variety of sexual stimuli just as they can learn to understand several languages.[10] All healthy children are born with capacity to learn any possible human language, and to adopt any possible human sexual behavior. From irua philosophy we have learned the importance of teaching children and youth about human sexuality.

Freud, in the *Sexual Enlightenment of Children* considered "whether children may be given any information at all in regard to the facts of sexual life." From a psychological view point, Freud identified dangers that result from hiding the truth about sex from children. He asserted that concealment of this reality lends a girl or boy to suspect the parents and grown-ups, and consequently the child's frank and genuine spirit of investigation is impaired. Furthermore, since the parents and the grown-ups are not trustworthy, the child rebels against the authority of their parents and later against every other form of authority. For Freud, covering the truth about one's sex life may result in a feeling of guilt with regard to sexual matters. Worse still, it may result in neurosis later on.

Teaching boys and girls and young men and women about human sexuality has been a problem for the last three decades. The battle against circumcision, which was started by the missionaries (who were aided and given legal right by the Colonial Administrators) in 1920s, 30s, and 40s eventually succeeded in getting rid of the initiation rituals and teaching about sex life. As the missionary culture was prevailing, and regarded as superior to African culture, the parent, who had not attended the missionary school, never bothered to teach their children about sexuality. They thought that the missionary schools, which had replaced the traditional ones, were holistic. They gave the children all the knowledge they needed. On the other hand, the school teachers and African catechists were not equipped to speak on this subject. Furthermore, since the missionary was opposed to all African dances and the circumcision of girls, the African catechists and teachers thought that they were opposed to all sexual behavior.

Thus neither the family institution nor the missionary institutions offered sex education. Concurrently, the 50s and 60s witnessed age-sets of youth who had not been schooled as far as sexual behavior is concerned. The only know-how of sex they had were the "don'ts." These age-sets are now the parents of the students in our secondary schools and colleges. Being victims of ambivalent attitudes toward sex, the age-sets had nothing positive to impart to their children in respect of sex life. Consequently, at present there is an outbreak of school-girl pregnancies. This problem, as the local papers have been reporting, is almost out of control in Kenya.

A good remedy for the above mentioned problems is sex education. Parents should teach children and adolescents about their reproductive systems. Parents should not be shy in answering children's questions about sexual life. They should, however, use simple language.

For instance, a child may see a male cat on top of a female cat and ask what is happening. The parents should tell the child about animal sexual behavior and reproductive systems and then move to the human reproduction system. They can also use the same visual aid to answer the most common question among children: *Where did I come from?* Children can relate what they observe in the animal kingdom to the human family. For example, a five year old boy happened to be with his mother while she was delivering. The boy stared at his mother until the baby was out. Astonished at seeing the placenta, the boy asked the mother: "Does it mean that human beings produce placenta like cows? " "Yes," replied the mother. This short genuine answer meant a lot to the boy. The boy's question indicates that children learn a great deal from the animal kingdom about sex life. It is also evident that even if the parents conceal the truth about sexual behavior, the animals will reveal it.

Parents should discuss with adolescents friendship between boys and girls, dating, engagement, marriage and contraceptives. The best time for this discussion is dinner time. The parent needs to bear in mind the fact that teenagers are living in a complex time and that the adolescents' era is different from that time when the parents were adolescents. The present youth are confronted by problems and temptations that were unknown during the parents' "good old days." For example, the seducing sugar daddies and sugar mammies were unheard of then. There was no temptation from the tourists. The taboos that guild the sexual behavior of the youth of the old days do not hold at present. Thus the discussion should also be focused on the new complexities. The issues about sugar daddies, sugar mammies, sex safaris, contraceptives, and family planning should be discussed. The parents should equip themselves on these subjects by reading some books about human sexuality. They should also draw from their wealth of experience.

Sex is not only an issue with children and adolescents. As noted earlier, it is an area of conflict in every developmental stage. Some women, after overcoming traditional sexual taboos, may reach the highest erogenous zone at their 30s, 40s, or even 50s. It may be at these stages, while the wife has the highest sexual appetite, that the husband is sublimating his sexual energy to his work. This un-evenness may be the major cause of marital conflict. Furthermore, women experience a great change during the menopause.

Men who are between forty and sixty are haunted by the fear of losing their potency. This fear may cause temporary impotence, or result in acting out their sexuality. The defense mechanism employed may include having an affair with the housemaid or a prostitute, or becoming a sugar daddy. Thus, the counselor should pay attention to the conflicts that are caused by sexuality in every stage of human development.

3. Sex as a Sacrament

The irua indicated that the pre-Puritan Gikuyu used sex as a sacrament. We have seen that initiation ceremonies started and concluded with a symbolic sex act. It was believed that sexual relationships expressed human and divine love at the deepest level. For the Gikuyu sexual intercourse was a sine qua non for a full religious life. In pre-marital counseling, we need to make it clear to young men and women that sex is not an illegitimate portion of the body. It is a means through which married couples express their deepest affection.

4. Sex as a Mark of the Rite of Passage

This book has also revealed the fact that sex marks the rites of passage. We have seen that most of mararanja songs praised sex organs and that it was the genitals that were circumcised. When pastoring and counseling, those who are going through the rites of passage—such as adolescence, betrothal, marriage, mid-life crisis, sublimation, bereavement, change of position and place—should be aware of the stage and how it affects their sexual behavior. As noted, when one is underwent the passage, he or she either became "oversexed" or "undersexed." Thus, instead of excommunicating a parishioner who is going through this crisis (as most African priests do), the priests should illuminate and help them to remain in their church community.

5. Sex and Loneliness and Distress

Sexuality was used as a means of the minimization of distress, sorrow, and loneliness. We saw that during the hukura ceremony, widows slept with their "sword sellers" and had full sexual intercourse twice. After the ceremony, the "sword seller" became a life-long sexual companion of the widow. This practice had both therapeutic and religious values.

Since the circumcised rarely shed tears, coitus was seen as an outlet for sorrow and a means of relaxation. Moreover, companionship enabled the widow to overcome her feeling of loss and loneliness. Religiously, it meant that God, who called the loved one, will continue to create other human beings. This act also stressed the fact that death was swallowed up by fertility. While the "sword selling" method is now past history, pastors and counselors should realize that the bereaved widows or widowers find it difficult to maintain their previous sexual discipline. It takes a long time to be adjusted and re-orientated. For this reason, he or she needs pastoral care and counseling. It is important to remember that a lonely, distressed, and sorrowful person needs our understanding and warm fellowship. However, as we shall see later, some Gikuyu driven by their collective unconscious, still use sexual intercourse as a means of coping with loss and loneliness.

6. Sex and Socialization

The initiation trained youth how to use sexuality as one of the means of socialization. It has been noted that after initiation, young men and women were given the freedom of feasting, dancing, and sleeping together, and of practicing platonic love. The opposite sexes were trained to live together as sexual partners. This is in keeping with the creation story, which tells us that "the Lord said, 'It is not good for the man to live alone. I will make a suitable companion to help him.'" The irua helped Gikuyu society to achieve this objective. It facilitated the creation of a society of male and female.

It is a pity that, at present, in the Gikuyu churches we have a men's side and women's side. The couple who live together and sleep in the same bed cannot sit together in the house of God because they are male and female. In Christian schools, youth are segregated according to their sexes. This is done in the name of Christ. This practice portrays Christ as an asexualized deity.

The New Testament knows nothing of asexualized Jesus. Rather, it witnesses to the logos who became sarx, all that which is human, and dwelt among us. As Tom Driver rightly contended, "A sexless Jesus can hardly be conceived to be fully human."[10] Jesus who is delineated by the Gospel writers, is more positive about human sexuality. He walked with women. He touched them and also allowed them to touch him. Jesus had a positive attitude toward those who were segregated because of "sexual sins." He told the Jewish priest, "I tell you this, tax gatherers and prostitutes are entering the kingdom of God ahead of you." As Leonard Hodson paraphrased, " Some tax gatherers and prostitutes are ahead of some of the clergy in the queue for heaven."[11]

We priests, should be more positive about human sexuality as was Jesus of Nazareth. It is my deep conviction that a Christianity, which segregates people according to their sex, is possibly a Christianity without Christ. To this end, when giving pastoral care and counseling to adolescents, we should pay attention to the physiological, psychological, and sociological conflicts which we have already discussed. We should remember that they are naturally bothered by the growth of their primary and secondary sex organs. Boys worry about the size of their penises, constant erections, and nocturnal emission, while girls are bothered by their breasts, pubic and auxiliary hair, and menstruation. We need to realize that sexual turmoil may cause neurosis and delinquency. Rather than maintaining the philosophy of sex segregation, which we inherited from the first African Christian generation (Mambere), we should bear in mind the fact that one of the major questions of adolescents is: *How can I relate to the opposite sex?*

The Church can deal with this issue by providing youth with a program that includes weekly meetings, youth rallies, and youth camps in which their questions can be listened to. Young people of both sexes should be trained and be allowed to live together—to walk together, to sing together, and play together. Better still, Church and school should teach them about friendship, courtship, sex, marriage, and parenthood.

7. *"NO" About Coitus*

Being a Christian theologian and psychologist, I cannot close this chapter without a "NO" about coitus. To do so, I would put Christianity at a lower level than the Gikuyu traditional religion. The Gikuyu custom did not allow young people to have a full sexual intercourse before marriage. They were given freedom of living their sexuality without acting it out. Christian culture, which is intertwined with African culture at present, does not advocate coitus among the youths. Most psychologists regard it as physically unhealthy for boys and girls to indulge themselves in an affair.

The view that young men and women may be sick if they don't have coitus cannot be supported by the recent research that has been done on human sexuality. While Freud categorized the sexual instinct with the survival instinct, the recent findings have challenged this categorization. For instance E. J. Haeberle[12] in *The Sex Atlas* argues that a sexual affair is not necessary for the survival of any organism. Lack of coitus is not the same as lack of food. A lack of food or liquid will lead to death, but a lack of sex has never killed anyone. Haeberle went on to contend that while lack of food intensifies the desire for food, the strength of sexual desire does not depend on the degree of sexual deprivation. Sexual abstinence does not always increase sexual desire and frequent sexual activity does not diminish it. On the contrary, some people who have been abstinent for a long time eventually lose all interest in sex, while others who are extremely active continue to be easily aroused. So young men and women can live without full sexual intercourse and remain mentally and physically fit. Unlike the pre-colonial youths, contemporary youths are not bound by taboos; for this reason we cannot restore traditional gwiko. This will only result in sexual immorality and pre-marital pregnancies.

Since we have a better understanding of human anatomy, I would strongly discourage modern girls from trimming their clitoris. I was privileged to interview women from several African countries who had attended the 4th General Assembly of the African Conference of Churches, which was held in Nairobi in August 1981. All of the women were against cutting of the clitoris. They contended that the practice was physiologically wrong and out of date. They, however, argued that initiation is still the best school for helping boys and girls to move from childhood to adulthood. For that reason, they argued that girls should undergo the rite without trimming the clitoris.

These ladies were right. For the clitoris is indeed a unique organ in the total of human anatomy, which gives women great pleasure during sexual intercourse. It is the seat of women delight (Realdo Colombo). Many women need direct clitoral stimulation in order to reach organism. The clitoris is also one of the most sensitive and most valuable parts of the sexual organ.

To this end, I would recommend an initiation similar to the one conducted by Edwina Johnson, which I mention earlier. We can also learn from the Diocese of Thika, which is under Episcopal oversight Dr. Gideon Githiga. Boys and girls are brought together to undergo vigorous teaching and training in responsible womanhood and manhood. After a week of training, girls are sent home. Boys are circumcised. When the boys heal, the girls are brought back so that they may graduate together and are all awarded Diocesan Certificate. This rite also prepares them for high School education.

Christian initiation should included training in godliness, morality, and Christian ethics. This should include teaching the youth to value their sexuality and to abstain from sexual immorality.

E. Summary

Since the theology and psychology of human sexuality is so complex, this chapter has only touched on the fringe of it. Although this subject has been dealt with from several perspectives, very little has been done from the perspective of African pastoral care and counseling. It is, therefore, hoped that there will be an extensive study on this subject. However, as this book has pointed out, we are sexual persons and sex is a gift from God, which can be used for God. Human sexuality is not an enemy of Christianity. Christians can live together as male and female. They can live and enjoy their sexuality by eating and drinking together, by touching and hugging each other, and by living together in a warm and cordial relationship. Sex, I believe, is one of the bases of the division of labor.

a

CHAPTER EIGHT

Division of Labor

This chapter will examine the traditional division of labor; how some duties were performed by a particular gender, how some works were discharged by both male and female as a part of a mutual celebration of life; and how the modern, professional, and technical society is experiencing tension caused by the contradictory teaching of a traditional teacher and a modern teacher. In addition, the chapter will afford you an invaluable opportunity to identify your personality type, and other types, and how each type performs particular services better or worse than other types.

As noted, irua initiated boys and girls into specific responsibilities and trained them how to perform particular jobs. They were told that an industrious child will never lack adoptive parents. Even if the parents die, this child will be reborn with a goat to another family, for society has a great interest in a productive person. They were informed that there was no work as big as an elephant, and the only work which is difficult is the unperformed work. They were made conscious of the fact that initiation ushered them to adult freedom, which was within the framework of the division of labor.

A. Division of Labor in Gikuyu Tradition

Since one was begotten as and to a community, responsibility to the community took priority over the service to an individual. An individual was first and foremost responsible to the nuclear family, which included parents, brothers, sisters, and half-brothers and half-sisters. By the same token, he worked for the extended family, which included grandparents, uncles, aunts, nieces, and nephews. By being both patrilineal and matrilineal, the Gikuyu expected the individual to be more obligated to the extended family of his lineage. For instance, because I belong to my mother's lineage, I herded my maternal grandfather's flock when I was a boy.

In addition to performing duties for the family, every initiated Gikuyu rendered some duty to his or her age group and gave assistance to the members of his clan. In most cases, this assistance was in the form of hospitality. For example, a wealthy man could allow a poor clan member to cultivate a portion of his land and put up a homestead.

Not only was an individual obligated to his or her primary groups, but every individual had territorial responsibilities. Every man and woman had definite duties to all the members of the village. These duties included fortification, protection and defense of the village. If called upon, he could also assist his neighbor in erecting a house, clearing the bush, and cultivating. A neighbor could count on sufficient assistance to build a house in a day or clear a large area for cultivation in a few days, without having to pay for the labor, except that he must supply the workers with a feast. He must also have initiated the work himself as a proof that he was not looking for help because he was lazy. He must also be someone who assists others. He who does not assist others is left alone with a proverb: "He who eats alone, dies alone."

When the expectant mother delivers, the neighboring women set a date on which they bring firewood, porridge, cooked food, sorghum, mallet, corn, sugar cane, sweet potatoes, and yams to the mother. In most cases, the mother of the newly born could get fuel and food supplies enough for three months. This gave her ample time for regaining her energy and nursing her baby without worrying about food and firewood for her family. Furthermore, an individual was a part of and responsible to the whole country. Duties to one's country included defense, building of bridges, and fire fighting.

Another major responsibility that every citizen had was related to religion. In time of drought, plague, and other calamities, the leading elders summoned all the people to gather together for worship. They then congregated under the Tree of God and gave sacrifice to the Great Provider. When killing the sacrificial animal, a boy, a girl, and a woman who has gone through menopause touched the animal's head while the elders slaughtered it and prepared and roasted the meat.

This was a symbolic act of inclusiveness and the community's total participation in the religious act. They then invoked the Ancient of the Day, a God who was worshiped by people of both sexes and of all ages. It was believed that faithful worship resulted in God's blessings for all. The blessing included gifts of rain, good harvest, health, unity, peace and prosperity, and vitality and capability of carrying out various responsibilities.

So inclusive were Gikuyu in religious act, that a family could not offer a sacrifice to God if one of their number was absent. If one of the family members was in a far country and unreachable, he was substituted by another person from the extended family or the neighborhood.

Customarily, there were duties that were performed by males and those which were done by females, as well as those which were wrought jointly by both sexes. Duties had nothing to do with the demonstration of superiority or inferiority, weakness or strength. Some of the jobs that were performed by women were too difficult for men. For instance, the Gikuyu women were trained (not by men but by women) from childhood to lift and carrying heavy things, such as firewood, in such a way that they built their muscles and were able to lift and carry heavier loads than men. This sounds awkward to the Western people. An American classmate and a great friend of mine shouted at me, "Shame on you!" for telling him that my mother could lift heavier objects than myself. He couldn't imagine how a fifty-eightyear-old woman could carry a heavier load than a man of thirty-four years of age.

A Gikuyu woman is not perceived by a Gikuyu male as psychologically or physically weak. Neither does she regard herself as a weaker object. There is a feeling of democracy and equality between the opposite sexes. This equality is not only evident in the division of labor, but also in the naming system. This is why children are named equally after paternal and maternal lineage. For instance, in our family, we are six. Three of us are matrilineal while the other three are patrilineal.

1. Man's Duty

As we have seen, during the weaning rite, the boy was made aware that he was growing to be a warrior. Hence, every Gikuyu male was a soldier. Military recruitment started after the initiation. The young man started by being a member of the junior regiment. At this initial stage, he had no direct responsibility or power. He was under the authority of the senior warrior regiment. After several years of training, he was promoted to the senior warrior regiment.

Apart from being a soldier, the Gikuyu male was a farmer. Men's work included cultivating the virgin land, bulldozing huge trees, cutting thick and thorny bushes, and working in the male gardens in which they grow male plantations, such as sugar canes, bananas, yams, tobacco, and sweet potatoes.

Likewise, men rolled or carried logs and heavy wood for erecting houses, building a bridge, or for fortification of a village. Men guarded the family and domestic animals against wild animals and the poachers from other tribes.

The elderly men and boys took animals to the pasture. It was also a male's duty to slaughter, roast, and distribute meat to the members of the family. They prepared and treated hides, which were used for making clothes, baby carriers, and beds. Metal work, carpentry, wood carving, and the making of bee hives were men's duties. The Gikuyu made superior spears, arrows, shields, and other ammunition, which were used by the warriors and also sold to the neighboring tribes, such as Masai and Wakaba.

2. Woman's Duty

A Gikuyu woman was tutored and trained for domestic and field work from the earliest stage of her life. As we have seen, during the weaning rite, the mother took the girl to the field where the latter ritually worked in the farm and carried small bundles of firewood. These were symbolic actions indicating that she was growing to work both in the house and in the field.

As it was with males, every female was an agriculturist. A married woman had her own farm and a granary storage. She had to produce enough food for her family and have a surplus, which she would to the market so as to buy other commodities were needed by the family.

In addition, women made a variety of earthenware, such as cooking pots and containers for alcoholic beverages, water, and grain. They weaved bags and baskets of numerous sizes, which were used for carrying grains, glossary, and other articles. They also plastered the walls of the house with clay and cow dung and painted it with white wash.

3. Duties Performed by Both Sexes

After initiation, there were more interactions between males and females. They feasted and socialized together. Since work was experienced as the celebration of life and socialization, there were some jobs which were performed jointly by men and women.

For instance, while men cultivated thick and thorny bushes, both sexes joined hands in breaking the ground, planting, weeding, and harvesting. Likewise, when erecting a house, the males did all the woodwork while women thatched the roof with the grass, but they both plastered the walls with mud.

Brewing of alcoholic beverages was performed by both sexes. However, men cut the sugar canes and heaped them together. Women carried them home and pounded them and men squeezed the pounded canes to produce juice, and then mixed the juice with honey and other ingredients in a big calabash. Both sexes drank beer together.

Trading and commerce were done by both males and females. Women sold and bought grains, earthenware, bags, and baskets, while men traded in domestic animals; working tools; weapons such as spears, bows, arrows and shields; and all wood and metal products. Both sexes and all ages, domestic animals, wild games, and the entire cosmic order participated in religious activities. These activities nurtured the inner and objective Tree of God and enhanced the community's harmony and cohesiveness.

4. Religious Duties

For the Gikuyu, as it is with other African people, religion was sine qua non to human life. Just as one cannot exist without air, water, and food, one cannot do without religion. Hence, it is axiomatic that every individual and the entire creation must participate in religious duties, worship, and ceremonies. It is impossible to perform any political, social, or military services without being involved in a religious ritual of some kind, because religion is life and life is religion. It permeates in all the departments of human life so fully that it is impossible to isolate it.

If a person refuses to cooperate in important religious rituals, he is forced by the family and neighbor to undergo through the rite. For instance, if a young man refuses to be circumcised, he is circumcised by force. Even in the modern technological society, if the Gikuyus discover that a particular man is not circumcised, they plot and confound him, and circumcise him by force. They'd rather risk to be imprisoned than to permit a male to stay uncircumcised.

In early days, if a person recanted religion and migrated to the town, he was disowned by his family and his community. .

Thus, religion permeates all that is, illumined political leaders and imbued the warriors with courage.

5. Political Duties

• Junior warrior regiment

After the initiation the male became not only a full grown person and a he-man but he also became a responsible member of society. His developmental title changed from kihii, a recipient or he-who-stretches-his-palm-to-receive to mwanake, my-son-take-the-weapon. He had to take the weapon and join the junior warrior regiment. His father gave him the armaments, which included a spear, a shield, and a sword. He was also provided with a sheep or a goat, which he used as fees to the warrior regiment school and a sacrifice to God. The animal was used for the ceremony, which entered the young man into warriorhood. His weapons were sprinkled with the blood of the sacrificial animal by the elder. He took an oath of allegiance and then the warriors feasted on the meat and then held a mock fighting.

After the ceremony, the junior warrior could go to war but had no power or authority. He was subordinate to the authority of the senior warriors and had no direct responsibilities. He acted as an acolyte or a server. During the warrior's dance, he couldn't dance on the stage, but performed outside the circle.

- Senior warrior regiment

After eighty-two moons, the junior warrior was promoted to senior warrior. He gave two goats or sheep as a fee for the rite of passage. the feast was followed by a big dance in which the warrior was permitted to dance in the inner circle. The ceremony ushered him to specific responsibilities and granted him the powers that go with the duties. He had authority over the junior warriors.

The regiment was governed by the councils. Territorially, there were village councils, district councils and the national council. Each of the councils was presided over by an elected president. The election of the presidents or judges was by consensus. There was no casting of votes. The leader was someone who possesses the spirit and the ideal of the community. He mirrored the ideals and aspirations of the group and had selfless dedication to the course of the village and national councils. He had to be someone who had demonstrated leadership qualities, impartiality in justice, bravery in war and discipline in a group.

The group leader represented his group to the village council; the village president represented the village to the district council, while the presidents of the district councils formed the national council of warriors. The leader of the warriors' councils also presented the interest of the young people to the elder's councils.

- The rite of passage to the senior eldership

As we have noted, the puberty rite was both a rite of passage for both the initiate and his or her parents. The initiate became a woman and a man while the parents were promoted to senior eldership. The parent moved from the stage of young adulthood to mature adulthood. The father moved from the state of a weapon-bearer to the bearer-of-the-sacred-leaves, from wearing the "military uniform" to wearing religious and political vestments (matathi). The mother moved from the state of being Kangei, young plant, to mature womanhood, Nyakinyua.

In this regard, when one had a boy or girl who was old enough to be circumcised, he was approached by the senior elders and was asked to prepare himself for the rite which was known as Gutonyio Keri, to be entered the second time, or the second rite of passage, which was to make him a bearer- of-the-sacred-leaves and the staff of the office. After getting the message from the senior elders, he consulted with the shaman. The shaman advised him about the right day for the occasion. The candidate then informed the village elders about the day a week before the appointed day.

In the morning of this day, the senior elders came and sat in the circle outside the house of the senior wife, who brought them food and drinks. Then the elders appointed two elders, who were to officiate the rite. Carrying their sacred leaves and staffs of office, the two elders entered the house and found the man and his wife seated at the fireplace. The man then brought a small calabash of beer, which was made out of hone and sugar cane. His wife brought a small beer-drinking horn. The four people sat around the fire.

One of the elders filled the horn with beer, sipped and spat over both his shoulders, and then poured a small amount of beer on the three stones that supported the cooking pot.

The beer was then passed over to the candidate, who sipped and then passed it over to his wife. He then communicated with ancestral spirits. This ritual conjoined the candidate with ancestral wisdom. They were connected with their genesis and then reintroduced to Gikuyu philosophy, which was embodied in idioms, proverbs, riddles, stories, and wise sayings.

After that was done, the four people chanted a prayer to God for the child who was about to be circumcised: "O, Ancient of the Day, the Ageless elder, God of our fathers, help our child to be successfully entered into Gikuyu wisdom, to grow in knowledge and in stature, to prosper and to bear many healthy children so as to perpetuate the family line.

Glory be to the Great Provider and peace to our children."

After the prayer, the man and his wife were sworn by the two elders to keep confidentiality of the senior elder's council. After this, the man was led out by the elders, walking between them, followed by his wife. The four entered into the circle and the man who had now become a senior elder greeted the elders, "My equal," (Wanjuwakine) and the elders responded in unison, "Our equal." After this, the wife returned to the house and brought a calabash of beer. She was also assisted by other senior women to bring food to the elders. The elders slaughtered a he-goat and dipped it's sexual organs into the blood and tied it on his wrist. This symbolized the fact that "Our equal" will never again be influenced by eros in making judgments, but will be led by logos, which was embodied in Gikuyu's idioms, proverbs, and wise sayings. Henceforth, he must be led by reason and wisdom and not by passion and pursue truth and justice at any cost.

After the ritual, the elder ate the roasted meat and drink the beer all the day long. From then on, the man who had become a senior elder never again greeted other senior elders in the usual Gikuyu greetings, "Wi mwega," (How is it?), but "Wanyuwakini," (My equal, or He who belongs to you at equal basis). These forms of greetings were solely reserved for those who were religiously, politically, and socially equal—the bearers of the sacred leaves and staffs of the office-athuri a matathi.

The duties of the senior elder included the study of Gikuyu philosophy and statues, peace-making, conflict management, advising the junior elders, attending senior elder's councils, offering sacrifices to God, and communicating with ancestors.

Since all the senior elders were equal, the Gikuyu did not have high priests, kings, or chiefs, but they had judges, who presided over the councils. A judge (Muthanaki) was a person who had leadership qualities, had demonstrated bravery in war, impartiality in judgment, devoted to the ideals of the community, was respected, and was taken seriously by all people. He was the most competent and diligent man in the age set and was capable of perceiving and articulating what was in the mind of the people. He had the audacity of and has mastered the whole gamut of people's political, social, and religious systems.

Even though the president was revered, he was not necessarily the wealthiest man. Unlike the modern westernized political leaders who buy their leadership and take it by the point of a gun, a traditional leader never bought his position with material things. He never campaigned and bribed people in order to win an election. By the same token, he never received bribery as to favor a particular person. He was elected because of his integrity and wealth of knowledge of people's democratic systems, which was based in circumcision and which stressed the individual's freedom to life, liberty, and property ownership with the full understanding that the government was by and for and of the people. He was aware that he was only first among equals and that his task was to create an atmosphere whereby justice could roll down like waters, and righteousness like an ever-flowing stream.

The Gikuyu democracy was more inclusive than that of the ancient Greeks. For unlike the Greek republic, which excluded women, aliens, and slaves from politics, the Gikuyu democracy embraced all those who were circumcised, regardless whether they were rich or poor.

As noted, people governed themselves through the councils. The first grade was the junior warrior's council, which was comprised of unmarried young men and women. The second grade was the senior warrior's council, which was composed of those who were married but did not have children and who were old enough to be circumcised. Young men, who belonged to this council, were known as spear-bearers and their councils was known as the council of weapon bearers. They were young fathers, who were still in the military. The female members of this council were known as young plants (Kangei). The role of this council was enforcement of community ethics to themselves and their juniors. They also congregated in the evenings for socializing, mutual friendly confrontation and brainstorming.

The third grade was the senior elder's council. This was for those elders, who carry the sacred leaves. This council dealt with important social, political, economical and religious issues.

Territorially, there were villages, local districts and country-wide councils. The senior elders' village councils included all men in the village who had been initiated to senior eldership and their wives and the presidents of junior and senior warriors' councils. The presidents of the warrior councils were allowed to speak only when they had to present cases of the warriors. Otherwise, they were expected to sit and listen to the elders, so as to learn how to deal with judicial deliberations when they became senior elders.

The presidents of the village councils formed the district council, while the presidents of district councils formed the country-wide council, which assembled at the

Gikuyu's "Garden of Eden" (Mukurwe wa Gathanga) whenever there were national issues.

Interestingly, Gikuyu democracy permitted the jurors to express both the unstructured and structured spheres of the psyche. When everyone had assembled, the president asked the elders to blow up or let the steam out (Kwibebeukia). Then they had a brief episode whereby everyone said whatever was on his mind and whatever was said at that time must go with the wind and could never be cited during the deliberation. After this episode, the judge then called the council into order. During this phase, everyone must be rational, logical, and must demonstrate integrity. The decisions were made by consensus. The Gikuyu, as it was with other African people, valued human relationships more than resolutions. In modern Kenya, modernized things are more prized than humanity. That being the case, most of the political leaders are elected because of their monetary possessions. After gaining power, which is without authority, they dip their fingers into the pockets of their electors. These poor politics have had bad effects on the economy, home, and family life. Kenya, as with other countries in Africa, south of the Sahara, has been politically shaken by colonization and decolonization. Colonization superimposed the West's political system on the continent, while decolonization left a mixture of African socialization and Western political systems. Africa, south of the Sahara, is in a liminal entity, between ethnocentricity and nationality, traditionality and modernity. As we shall see in the following pages, the family's aircraft is flying in the turbulent atmospheric conditions of change. Yet, we strongly believe that even though there are dying elements, a very healthy child will be born by this continent, which is the mother of all humanity.

B. Division of Labor and Family in Transition

The division of labor in Kenya and Africa, south of the Sahara, has to be observed against the background of dichotomies experienced by the modern African. There are dichotomies between tradition and modernity, urbanization and ruralization, literacy and illiteracy, Christianity and Islam versus traditional religions, tribilization and nationalization, traditional political systems and political idealisms borrowed from the Western hemisphere, African social systems and the growing social stratification that is being adopted from the West, and authoritarianism and absolution versus African freedom of expression, which was fostered by the age-grouping systems.

The Africans are somewhat hovering in the air looking for firm ground on which to settle. They are between time. There is something that is ebbing, declining, dying, and decaying. Nevertheless, a fully developed embryo is vibrating, breathing, and kicking in the African womb. It's name, nature, form, and character are unknown.

I perceived this fetus when I was conducting marriage seminars in various places in Kenya. The group ranged from thirty to five hundred. The questions for discussion were: *What spoils the relationship between a husband and a wife today? What should the marriage partners do to improve their relationship?* The groups identified a number of issues that were affecting an individual's role in the family and society. It was observed that we are moving from a patriarchal society to a matriarchal society, or democratization of the genders; children who were traditionally the parent's assets and wealth are now becoming liabilities; the husbands who were ever in the homesteads in the father's house are migrating from the homesteads to the cities and towns, leaving their wives in the countryside with the disproportional burden of family care; alcoholic beverages, which were customarily taken during special celebrations, have become daily drinks for men and women who are suffering from spiritual emptiness; drugs, which were unheard of by our forefathers, are becoming rampant; money and the economy is changing both the philosophy of life and concept of time; and the marriage partners and single parents who have careers have left their children in the hands of teenage-maids.

1. Movement from a Patriarchal Society to a Matriarchal Society

As we have seen, initiation introduced a democratic system in the family and community. The father was, however, the chairman or head of the family. The mother, on the other hand, was trained from childhood on how to turn the "head." To use the words of the Mother's Union, she was the "neck" of the "head." She was a strong backbone of her husband. She tactfully and unconsciously turns the "head." But all of a sudden, she has become a "neck" without a "head." The "head" has moved from the homestead in the rural areas to the city for salaried jobs. Some fathers visit their families once a month, others once a year, while some never come back home. Research, which was conducted by Nairobi University, estimated that 60 percent of the husbands in Kenya are absentee husbands.

Some husbands who stay with their families tend to ignore domestic responsibility if their wives are professional with better salaries than the husbands. As one wife complained during the marriage enrichment seminar, "Although my husband has a job, I am totally responsible for the family. Not only do I have to feed, clothe and educate the children, but I also have to feed and clothe my husband. At first, I was outraged, since I never saw my mother playing this role. But I gradually regarded my husband as one of my boys. This conviction gave me a peace of mind. Nevertheless, it gets on my nerves, whenever he shouts at me." Thus, most wives are both the breadwinners and the managers of their home. It is estimated that two-thirds of the grains in Africa, south of the Sahara, is produced by women.

A few young husbands, particularly those who are brought up by the single mothers, have accepted the leadership of their wives. As one young man said to his fiancé during premarital counseling: "I was brought up by my mother. She was the head of the family. I don't know what it is for a man to be the head of the family and for that reason, don't expect me to head our family. Lead and I will follow."

However, even if the husband or the wife accepts his position, this does not always solve the problem, since one sphere of the family is patriarchal. A wife with an irresponsible husband may have a neighboring family with a very responsible husband and she may constantly compare her condition with that of her neighbor and thereby suffer from a relative deprivation.

2. Children are Becoming Liabilities

Customarily, children were regarded as a great asset by the parents because of the fact that they constituted the work force. After becoming grown up, they performed domestic work, cared for livestock, and worked in the farm. The young warriors raided other tribes and captured their cattle, goats, and sheep, which they brought to their parents. The young women were given for marriage and the parents received the bride's prize in return. Currently, the parents are financially supporting their children (without receiving anything in return) until they are through with their primary, secondary and college education. Since the parents regard educated children as a great investment, they rid them of any duty that could interfere with their studies. The parents from middle and upper classes employ house maids to do all the chores so as to allow their children to give their undivided loyalty to academic work. They do this with the anticipation of getting a lion's share in economic benefits, which their children will attain after graduating from college and are employed in well-paying jobs. On the contrary, by being over-indulged and ever-receiving from the parents without reciprocating, some modern young adults have become eternal parasites to their parents. They continue making heavy demands on their family, even after getting employment. Some have sued their aging fathers so as to force them to relinquish the family property to them. The first born of a lay-reader of a church that I ministered at in Kenya filed a lawsuit against his father alleging that his father was an alcoholic and was intending to sell his land through the influence of alcohol. The young man wanted the court to authorize the transfer of the title deed to him. However, his father, who only sipped wine once a week during the Holy Communion, was found innocent. But, he was terribly hurt by being sued by his son, whom he has reared and educated. In some cases, the fathers have been murdered by their pampered sons as they attempted to acquire their father's property. Thus, children who were their parent's life insurance in the past have become unbearable monsters. These parasites have depleted and exhausted their parents. They have broken their hearts and have inflicted a sharp, thin pain in their guts.

3. Interferences from In-Laws

According to the passing generation, a young man built a house away from his parents before or after marriage. Never did he live in the same homestead with his parents after marriage. This set-up enabled him to build a separate and independent nuclear family.

Presently, due to scarcity of land, some young couples live in the same homestead and use the same gate with their parents. In addition to that, some wealthy parents employ their sons to either work in their farms or operate their business. Consequently, these parents regard their sons and daughter-in-law as their possession. If the daughter-in-law is a career woman, the "big daddy" expects her earnings to come to the main pool. If the son leaves for work in the town and stays away from his family, the "big daddy" may become a "big husband" to his daughter-in-law and have an affair with her—a behavior which was regarded as an outrageous incest taboo in the old days.

During the marriage seminars, the young wives who were victims of the systems, expressed their resentments with the following statements, "Never shall I accept to be absorbed by the in-laws." "I have no problem with my husband, but I am constantly offended by his father's interference and authoritarianism." "Unless my husband moves away from that homestead," lamented a young woman who had returned to her parents, "I shall never go back to that home." "My husband forms a coalition with his parents against me," complained a young school teacher. "I am tired, fed-up, and burnt out for using too much energy in self-defense. I cannot stand it anymore." These women felt over-worked, exploited, and abused. The situation may worsen if the husband moves to the city for job opportunity and leaves his wife and children in the countryside.

4. Absentee Husbands and Division of Labor

Customarily, a husband lived in a hut, which was situated in the homestead near the main gate in order to guard the family and the livestock. There, his children went for advice. His wives visited him for sexual gratification. But, the bad news is that westernization, urbanization, and job opportunities have moved the father's house from the homestead to the city. As we have noted, some husbands come home once a month, others once a year, and others after a decade, while others never come back home. This phenomenon of absentee husbands is prevalent in Africa, south of the Sahara. It is also a trend in the West Indies. During my visit to Barbados, I learned that most husbands are either in the United Kingdom or the United States for job opportunities. They leave their wives and children on the Island, and in most cases, the husband never comes back home. The mother has to provide, protect, and guide her children. It is also estimated that 70 percent of the African American families in the United States are headed by a mother. The mother is not only the head of the household, but she is also the provider. In some cases, the African American mother is over-worked, burnt out, depleted, and battered. The African American father does not voluntarily abandon his family responsibility, but has been forced by the evil forces, which have been afflicting him for over three hundred years. No father's ego has been as severely mutilated as the black father's in the United States. Even though he has made enormous contributions in the American society, in science and technology, being the mayors of major cities, being American ambassadors to the United Nations, being the top soldiers (like Colin Powell), being the judge of the Supreme Court (like Clarence Thomas), being innovators and discoverers—he is still regarded as the embodiment of evil. He is witch-hunted more than any other human. Society puts a magnifying glass on his birthmark or his blind spots and turn a blind eye to the superior side of his personality. He never hears anything positive either about himself or his father land. The media tells him constantly that he's in prison, on drugs, a murderer, irresponsible, and accused of other vices. The harder he endeavors to humanize humanity, the more he is dehumanized; the more he enriches the society, the more he is impoverished; the more he protects, the more he is attacked; the more he tries to build, the more his ego is demolished. The African American father is a victim who is regarded as and punished as a criminal. He is, indeed, caricatured and then lynched. His suffering is the suffering of the black mother and her family.

For when he is psychologically incapacitated, he strikes the nearest and the safest object—the black mother. Statistically, there are more black wives, who are beaten up by their husbands than white wives. They beat them because of low-self-esteem, which is inflicted on them by the society and pent-up anger generated from work and social environments. By being smothered from childhood to adulthood by the Great Black Mother, the black male's avenues to responsible partnerships are blocked. And, thus, the black mother has to shoulder all the family's burden.

Nevertheless, we have "seven thousand black fathers" who have triumphantly liberated themselves from the status of eternal boyhood. They have allowed their roots to penetrate deeper to their fatherland thereby drawing ego energy from the African Great Father and Great Mother. They have stretched their alms over the Atlantic Ocean and have reached out to Ethiopia, their mother land. Rather than being ashamed of being identified by their motherland, these fathers are actively re-Africanizing the de-Africanized sphere of the African Americans. These fathers are responsible marriage partners. They are sought after as precious jewels for political, societal and ecclesiastical leadership. They are the messiahs of the African American boys. And since they knew where the shoe pinches, they are nurturing the egos of these boys and are helping them to travel on the road that leads to responsible manhood. By re-Africanizing, humanizing, and Christianizing these black males, the "seven thousand black fathers" are creating dependable marriage partners for the African American wives.

Paradoxically, these messiahs are advocating schools for Negro boys. These schools will shield the boys from the smothering of the Great Black Mother, which suffocates their ego and the external environments, which give the black male distorted self-images and negative attitudes toward their roots. In addition to the Humanities, Math, Science, and Technology, the curriculum of these schools will include reading of autobiographies and biographies of the African and the American African heroes. They will study African religions and philosophy, African psychology, and African culture. They will have daily physical and mental exercises. Mental exercise will include debate, discussion, and friendly confrontation. They will be trained on how to turn a deaf ear to negative propaganda against African descent. They will be trained how to discard gossip, damaging allegations, witch-hunting of African American religious and political leaders.

They will be enticed to look at Africa as their Jerusalem, Garden of Eden, and cosmic center. They will be tutored on human relationship, how to relate with women, home and family life, how to build and abide in the father's house (Thingira) in order to offer protection and security to the African American mothers. They will indeed become a great asset to the Negro mother and her children.

These "seven thousand African American fathers" have discovered that they are mighty eagles with strong wings and the ability to fly into the cosmos. They are enabling the African American children to discover and use their strong wings. They are training them how to use their strong wings for flying to the world of freedom and prosperity.. They are imbuing their spirits with self-determination. They give them the water of life, which is filling their lives with vitality and ability to make their own choices. They are preparing young men and women for responsible parenthood.

Back to Africa. The borrowed, unsuccessful, Western, political, and economic systems, which are superimposed on the African continent, are affecting the personality of the African father. The African father is expected to be a breadwinner. The fathers who are unsuccessful in winning the bread are also losing their egos. Some of these fathers who are living with their families are retreating to drug and alcohol dependence. They go out to the pubs for drinks and return home late at night when the children are asleep and leave. for work very early in the morning before they have seen their children. This habit has led to infidelity and irresponsibility.

In reaction to this problem, some women (including Christian women) have turned to the traditional medicine man. The latter has discovered a medicine, which the former puts in her husband's drink or food. This medication is intended to make the husband docile, domesticated, and everbound to his wife and home, but unfortunately, most men who are served with these ingredients have become both docile and mentally retarded. Some women have regretted this and gone back to the medicine man for a cure. One wife had this dialogue with a doctor."

"After taking the medicine, my husband became mentally sick and lost his job. I need a cure for his mental disability."

"I have the medicine for docility and domestication," answered the medicine man, "but I have no medicine for neutralization." The woman was angry and disappointed realizing that she will now take care of her retarded husband as one of her children. Many a husband in the areas are harbored with the fear of being served with this stuff.

However, we still have a large number of African husbands who are dedicated and committed to their families. These fathers are found both in urban and rural areas. Likewise, we do have committed and faithful mothers. The majority of these mothers and fathers are Christians. They are more cooperative and corroborative than pre-Christian African parents. They are and will be the strong backbone to the emerging generation.

Nevertheless, these committed couples are being challenged by family responsibility, particularly if both of them are professionals with full-time jobs. They are left with no time for their children. The house maids are in charge of the children.

5. *House Maids*

Africans have employed men and women servants since time immemorial. They hired them for domestic work, farming, and herding. They gave them separate huts, and for that reason, a servant couldn't interfere with the nuclear or extended family. While women servants were deployed for domestic work and child care, they never substituted the parents.

In contrast, the modern maids are as substitute mothers, whose duties include child care and most of the household chores. They live under the same roof with their masters. Their presence in the house and absence of the mother has resulted in infidelity, separation, and divorce. Since most of the maids are teenage girls, who have no training in child care, most of the children are abused and undernourished. Some maids have brought calamity to children and strife in marriage. A few husbands have divorced their wives and married their maids.

In one seminar, there was a heated debate on the quality and personality type of a maid that the couples should employ. A young woman, who was a school teacher said, "I advise my husband to get me the ugliest girl in the village. This solves the problem of infidelity." "There is no ugly woman in the dark," a man with a seductive smile interjected. This man was supported by a middle-aged woman, who was an ex-house servant. We burst into laughter as she narrated her experience.

"I am a very ugly woman, who had been employed as a maid by people from varied social strata—wealthy business men, medical doctors, and university professors. None of these men have not seduced me. The worst of them all was a professor, who constantly persuaded me to go out with him to a movie. But, I categorically refused. He enticed me with a lot of money, but I never yielded. Though I am a woman of the lowest class and very ugly, the professional husbands didn't mind. But, I stood firm because I had Christ. So the answer to this problem is not ugliness but Christ."

While Christ is the answer to sexual morality, it is simplistic to suggest that he is the answer to the division of labor as it relates to the maid-wife-husband triangle. The ugly maid is not an answer, either. She is but an ugly substitute mother who will develop a child with ego deflation or poor self-image. With threatening inflation and worsening economy, it is unrealistic to expect a career woman to stay at home to take care of the children. As we have seen, African mothers were not confined in the kitchen and domestic work. They fully participated in agricultural, commercial and religious duties. As with the case of Wanqu wa Makeri, the women were warriors and judges.

But the modern technological and professional society demands a system that would give professional care to the African child. We need daycares, which run from 6:00 a.m. to 6:00 p.m. These daycares should employ mature men and women who have done some studying in child psychology. The working parent should take their children to the daycare in the morning as they go to work and pick them up in the evening after work. While mothers should remain masters of domestic work and child's care, men should learn how to assist and fill-in. They should fight a mythological demon, which maintains that it is only a mother who can both nurse a baby and change diapers. These rituals bind the baby to the father and may save a baby boy from being homophobic. But more importantly, the mother and the father will share the duties that are performed by the maid. They will be free from the presence of an outsider who invades their privacy, and disrupts their marriage, and abuses their children. Involvement of both parents in house chores and rearing of children will develop a healthy Great Mother and Great Father in the offspring's personality. More about this on the chapters on Great Mother and Great Father.

In career choices, however, we must go beyond traditional African philosophy of division of labor. We will need illumination of the modern psychology. According to analytical psychology and Myers-Briggs personality typing, there are women who can adequately perform the duties that the ancient man attributed to males, and males who can do better duties that were ascribed to women. There are women, who like Wangu, can be able judges political and religios leaders. In this section, you have a blessing of learning how to identify your types and other types. You will then fall in love with yourself and others. After enjoying what you are and being what you are you will let others be without trying to form them in your own image.

C. Psychology and Division of Labor

Immediately following my matriculation at the School of Theology at the University of the South in the Summer of 1976, I was told that we had to do a psychological test. At that time, I had a real problem of finding places, and for that reason, I was ten minutes late for the test because I couldn't find where the class was. I was poor in observation and getting the details of the landmarks, since I was pre-occupied with intuition, I was always thinking about something, developing an idea rather than watching my direction. I was more interested in the inner world more than the outer world. I focused more to the horizon than to where I was stepping. More often than not, I had to stumble on something as I walked. So, even though we had been shown where the class was during the orientation, it took me time to figure out where the examination was located.

After finding the class, I was very nervous and feeling guilty for being late. I hated and still hate being late. The professor handed over to me a paper, which appeared to me as if it had five hundred questions. I answered all the questions. But, I was apprehensive about the whole business of psychoanalysis. After the test, I refused to go to check out my type. I contended that there is no human laboratory which is scientific enough to analyze human beings since personality is as complex as life itself. I stayed at the University of the South for three years without checking my type. I associated type-matching with Analytical Psychology, which I disliked at the time, because everybody at the seminary was talking about C. G. Jung.

After finishing the Master of Divinity program, my wife and I audited a class on Jung under Professor Craig Anderson, who was my professor of pastoral psychology. I took the class, not because I was interested in Jung, but for my admiration of Craig. Mysteriously, anything that

Craig recommended, I took it without reservation. My book shelves were full of books recommended by him. I never understood why I identified with him so much, even though he had almost no personal contact with me. On one occasion he was confronted by the students for giving them too much work. To my surprise, I felt as though it was I who was being attacked.

Professor Anderson asked the class to take the MyersBriggs Type Indicator Test. Since I could not say no to him, I cooperated. It turned out that I was an INTJ. Craig, my favorite professor, was also an INTJ. My dear wife was an INFJ. Since that period, I developed an interest in C. G. Jung and the Myers-Briggs Type Indicator. Although MyersBriggs psychology is not scientific enough to explain the mystery of human personality, it is the best tool for helping us to know what we can do better and how our gathering and processing of data is influenced by our preferences and temperaments.

In the 1950s, Katheryn Briggs, with her daughter, Isabel Myers, illuminated by C. G. Jung's work on "psychological types," observed that there are sixteen personality types. Each of these types prefers particular patterns of action and approaches to life in his/her own way. Because of the varied temperaments and preferences, each type possesses his/her own mode of life, ways of interacting with people, and has the potential for specific duties. The differences in behavior are the results of preferences, which emerge early in life.

According to Myers-Briggs, there are four pairs of contrasting preferences. These are: Extroversion(E) vs. Introversion(I), Sensing(S) vs. Intuition(N), Thinking(T) vs. Feeling(F), Judging(J) vs. Perceiving(P). Each person develops four of the preferences while the other four remain less developed. One operates on all preferences, but the preferred preferences are as naturally employed just as the right-handed person uses the right hand more naturally than the left hand. The variation in combinations of the preferences result to sixteen personality types. These are: ISTJ, ISFJ, INFJ, INTJ, ISTP, ISFP, INFP, INTP, ESTP, ESFP, ENFP, ENTP, ESTJ, ESFJ, ENFJ, ENTJ.[11] Each of these types plays a particular role better than the other and has also some aspects that are inferior to other types. Although society tends to prefer and even reward some types more than others, none of the types are more useful than others. If an organization lacks one of the types, it tends to have some defects. Thus, all types are of equal value in the scheme of the division of labor.

1. Your Preferences

In order to enjoy this section, you need to identify your type by putting a check mark on those statements that applies to your preferences. Then count your scores. The high score is an indication of your dominant function. If, for instance, you score 19 points in E and 10 points in I, this means that you are an Extrovert. If you score the same points on both contrasting preferences, this indicates that you have either developed both preferences or you are not clear about your preferences. If you are not clear about your preference, you may want to read these statements with a friend who knows you well and get feedback from him/her.

However, the best means of getting an accurate knowledge of your type is by taking the Myers-Briggs Type Indicator Test (MBTI) administered by authorized counselors or psychologists.

a. Extrovert vs. Introvert

Extrovert

You are an Extrovert(E) if:

1. you like talking in and to a group
2. you speak first, think later
3. things become clear as you talk
4. you have numerous friends
5. your battery is charged by people
6. you feel empty if you stay alone for a long time
7. you listen with your mouth open
8. you constantly need affirmation
9. you dominate conversations most of the time
10. you prefer being outside with people than alone or with a few people
11. you have a large number of friends
12. you are approachable
13. you enjoy being interrupted by a telephone call
14. you enjoy a surprise visit by a friend
15. you dominate a conversation in a group
16. you are comfortable interacting with strangers
17. the more you stay with people at a party, the more your energy increases
18. you are well-informed about what is happening in your social groups

19. you prefer many friends with brief contact
20. in a group, you initiate a conversation

Introvert

You are an Introvert(I) if:

1. you like talking to one person rather than a group
2. you think before you talk
3. you can focus on an issue better when you are alone
4. you have a few intimate friends
5. you charge your battery by being alone
6. you become restless if you stay for a long time at a party
7. you leave a meeting saying, "Why didn't I say it?"
8. you are not easily approachable
9. when the telephone rings, you prefer someone else to pick it up
10. you can keep a secret
11. you don't dominate a conversation in a group
12. you don't like talking to a stranger
13. you can concentrate on something for a long time
14. you are very careful in choosing your friends
15. you are a better listener
16. at a party, you interact with a few friends
17. at a party, you leave early with lesser energy
18. you rehearse what you have to say before you say it
19. some people say you are shy or reserved or private
20. you like giving general answers

b. Sensor vs. Intuitive

Sensor

You are a Sensor(S) if:

1. you are interested in the little things of everyday life
2. you like facts
3. you are more interested in reality than possibility
4. you are more interested in actual than possible
5. you are not interested in imaginary things
6. you prefer actual examples to hypothetical examples
7. you dislike visionaries
8. you are more interested in doing useful things
9. you are more interested in production and distribution than in research and designs
10. you are more practical than frank and open
11. you are more sensible than imaginative
12. you prefer identifying yourself with others than using them
13. you are more concerned about the present than the future
14. you prefer fact to fantasy
15. you are more practical than ingenious
16. you prefer specific answers to general answers
17. you wonder why people keep on improving things that do not need improvement
18. you prefer facts and figures to ideas and theories
19. you are uncomfortable when you don't get details and clear instructions

20. as an interviewer, you would be more interested in the interviewee's experience, than in her speculation of the future of the organization

Intuitive

You are an Intuitive(N) if:

1. you are goal-and-future orientated
2. you are more theoretical than practical
3. you are more imaginative than factual
4. you are more concerned with possibilities than reality
5. if you wish that people would express what they say by the use of analogy
6. you are interested in dreams and fantasies
7. you are interested in design and research rather than production and distribution
8. you find it uncomfortable identifying with others
9. you like thinking and doing several things at once
10. you are more interested in where you are going more than where you are
11. you are bored by the details
12. you like reading between the lines
13. you don't like accepting things at face value
14. you like giving general answers to most questions
15. you are interested in finding the relationship between things
16. you prefer saying: "about," "probably," "approximately"
17. if, when asked about time, rather than giving the actual time, you say, "about time," "it is too early,"

"time to go home," and you get irritated when pressed for specific times

18. people accuse you of being absent-minded and of not seeing things, but you know you only see what you need to see

19. if you miss your car in a parking lot or lose your pen when it is in your pocket

20. if you think of yourself as innovative rather than practical

c. Thinkers vs. Feelers

Thinker

You are a Thinker(T) if:

1. you are accused of being hard-headed (Kichwa Ngumu)
2. you think what to feel
3. you can remain objective and calm while everybody else is subjective and emotional
4. you are more concerned with facts and fairness than people's feelings
5. you like looking at both sides of an issue
6. in arguments, you are more concerned with increasing your knowledge than winning an argument
7. you are accused of being detached and aloof
8. you are proud of your ability of being objective
9. you were skeptical about taking this test, but took it when you learned that it is beneficial

10. you would still work with the people who do not like you, for what matters to you is the benefit you get from the job and you like comforting yourself with a Gikuyu proverb, "The eyes of the frogs don't prevent a cow from drinking some water"

11. you don't understand why people get angry for business which doesn't concern them and you challenge them with a Swahilii proverb, "Why bother yourself with hot pepper which isn't in your mouth?"

12. you don't mind making and implementing difficult decisions

13. you value logic more than feelings

14. you become uncomfortable when people around you become emotional

15. you like arguing for the sake of arguing

16. you become uncomfortable with people who cannot take a strong stand

17. you are embarrassed by excessive expressions of feelings

18. you like winning people to your point through logic rather than emotions

19. in your judgment, you are more influenced by laws and principles than circumstances

20. you would like people to be guided by logic than by feelings

Feeler

You are a Feeler (F) if:

1. you are more concerned with values than principles

2. you prefer persuasion to firmness
3. you prefer arriving at an agreement on an issue than discussing it thoroughly
4. you are more personal than impersonal
5. you are more humane than just
6. you maintain that human beings are more valuable than laws and norms
7. you see yourself as soft-hearted
8. you are sympathetic
9. you are more comfortable with personal judgment than impersonal judgment
10. you perceive people who don't care about others feelings as cold, heartless, and stone-hearted
11. you enjoy expressing your feelings
12. you like winning people over to your side by appealing to their feelings and emotions
13. you believe that people's feelings are more important than decisions
14. you like pleasing and accommodating others
15. you value human relationships more than principles and laws
16. you are accused of being double-faced for your attempts to please both sides
17. you don't mind swallowing your own words, if you discover that they have offended someone
18. your friends complain that you take things too personally
19. you don't like engaging yourself in any activity that hurts other people's feelings
20. in your judging of others, you are more influenced by circumstances than law and principles

d. Judgers vs. Perceivers

Judgers

You are a Judger(J) if

1. you prefer setting a goal
2. you move toward the goal
3. you are decisive
4. you implement the resolution
5. you do not want to leave things hanging in the hair
6. you are on time most of the time
7. you are always uncomfortable when people arrive late
8. you like making and following the time table
9. you don't rest until everything is in its place
10. you don't like surprises
11. you like listing what you are planning to do before you do
12. you make your choice carefully
13. you are bothered when things are incomplete
14. people accuse you of being too serious
15. when stressing a point people thing you are angry even when you are not
16. you prefer an orderly life
17. you like doing things on purpose
18. you are intentional
19. you have a fixed and a regular way of doing things
20. you are uncomfortable when people do things without aim or purpose.

Perceiver

You are perceiver(P) if:

1. you like to wait and see philosophy
2. you are flexible
3. you easily adapt to a situation
4. you are spontaneous
5. you hate deadlines
6. you are accused of being repetitious
7. people complain that you are aimless
8. some people perceive you as procrastinator
9. you are easily drawn to some things or someone.
10. you love exploring the unknown
11. you like fun
12. you like options
13. you don't mind doing things at the last minute
14. you suddenly act without caring the consequences
15. you are not bothered when things are not completed
16. you are more easy going and serious
17. you prefer being merciful than just
18. you are open minded.
19. you don't care to think carefully before you speak
20. in a group, you are also spontaneous

In the following pages, we will examine each preference and each of sixteen personality types and how the Africans use naming, nicknaming, expressions, and proverbs to typify the personality.

2. Naming

If you are an Extrovert, the African may nickname you *maneno (*words) or *mwaria njarie* (he who repeats what has already been said) or *kanua kahiu (*hot mouth) or *Nyaguthia (*she who is here and there).

3. Sixteen Personality Types

a. ISTJ

If you are an ISTJ, you constitute 6 percent of the population. You are objective, concrete, pragmatic, decisive, dependable, and dedicated. You have a great sense of responsibility and you are good at dealing with people. These qualities make you excel both at school and work. You can be a good community leader, project manager, soldier, surgeon, lawyer, accountant, planner, organizer, controlling officer, auditor, treasurer, tax examiner, legal secretary, or high school teacher. The Gikuyu proverb, "An industrious child never lacks adoptive parents," refers to you.

b. ISFJ

If you are an ISFJ, you belong to 6 percent of the population. Even though you appear quiet, reserved, down-toearth, and easy-going; you are sensible, orderly, neat, gentle, steady, humane, sociable, dutiful, obedient, traditional, and super-dependable.

You can be a good primary school teacher, nurse, librarian, health technician, secretary, general medical practitioner.

You can be superb in a middle-management job dealing with the "boss" and subordinate staff, the needy, marginalized, and ignorant people.

c. *INFJ*

If you are an INFJ, you will find only one person out of a hundred who possesses your clay. You are invaluable, yet unfathomable, misinterpretable, misunderstandable, warm, enthusiastic, cooperative, marked with originality, and capability of implementation of resolutions. You can, indeed, be an excellent student, psychologist, psychiatrist, medical doctor, church minister, writer, or researcher. You can be a priest and a king maker. You can tackle complex issues and deal with difficult people.

d. *INTJ*

If you are an INTJ, like your brother INFJ, there is one of your kind in every hundred people. Likewise, you are more concerned in understanding than being understood. You are accused of being obscure, cold, reserved, aloof, unresponsive. Yet, you are the most independent of all types. You are innovative, futuristic, pragmatic, a theoretician, and goal-oriented. You have the natural propensity for discerning the nature of the whole flock and of distinguishing characteristics and the need of individual sheep. By being a high achiever (type A) and splendid organizer, you are capable of being at the top of the pyramid of any organization. You can become a successful managing director, chief executive officer, university professor, researcher, inventor, program director, analyst, physical scientist, curriculum developer, and writer.

e. ISFP

If you are an ISFP, you are accused of being bura matu, an earless animal, a slow learner, a day-dreamer, quiet, reserved, and uncompetitive. While there may be some truth to some of these accusations, you know you are misunderstood.

You are indeed the most misunderstood and most invisible of all types. For you know for sure that you are cheerful, optimistic, fraternal, trusting, and generous. You have the intrinsic propensity for nature, wild life, and children. Because of your love for freedom, you are not interested in controlling or influencing others or being conventional or keeping a boring routine. Your free spirit enjoys excitement, taking risk, and choices. Professionally, you can excel in fine art-music, dance, graphic art, needlepoint, crocheting, auto-mechanics, cosmetology, carpentry, psychology, veterinary science, botany, theology, sociology, and bookkeeping.

There is 6 percent of your type in the general population.

f. ISTP

If you are a female ISTP, you might remember how your parents and other people used to shout at you when you were growing up, "Wanja Kahii," little girl who is like a boy. And, being an introvert, people complain that you are reserved, aloof, detached, unpredictable, insubordinate, and reckless. Yet, even though they try to put you down, you neither complain nor lose heart because you know your strength. You know that you are the most artistic of all types. You are spontaneous, humorous, handy, and endowed with the enormous ability of handling the unexpected and fixing the unfixable. Like an eagle, you fly high to observe that which is going down the drain, and before it vanishes, you descend like a lightning bolt and save the situation to the surprise of all other types. After you have fixed the unfixable, rather than calling you Wanja Kahii, they call you Kabunja ndua—he who breaks a ceremonial calabash of beer as he hastens to rescue the perishing. You are indeed a splendid hero and you know it.

Even if you are a female, you can do a man's job. Farm men's crops and engage in men's trades. Both males and females are good at handicrafts, mechanics, masonry, carpentry, engineering, armed forces, auto racing, and driving heavy machinery, like rockets, bulldozers, trucks, lorry buses, and mobile homes. You indeed possess substance of the Great Father.

g. INFP

If you are a male INFP, you remember people shouting at you, "Nyukwa," your mother, he who looks like a female. You were accused of being easy-going, soft, too gentle, wimpy. People tend to misunderstand you because there is only one of your type in every hundred people. Yet, you don't become disoriented by the external voices because you have a better self-knowledge than all other types. You are the best at self-identity, self-definition, self-dedication, selfsacrifice, and self-depreciation. You are calm, compassionate, idealistic, warm, **and a** parent-teacher pleaser. You are better in higher studies than primary and secondary studies. Unlike other types, you are your own arch critic. Please try to be fairer to yourself because you are great. I know you are glad to know that Abraham Lincoln (one of the Greatest American presidents, who fought for the emancipation of slaves) and Isabel Briggs Myers (who developed the personality types theory) were your type. With regard to the division of labor, you can be a psychologist, psychiatrist, church minister, rabbi, missionary, writer, artist, editor, social worker, and family doctor. Whether you are a male or a female, you have a good supply of the qualities of the Great Mother.

h. *INTP*

If you are an INTP, you enjoy using Gikuyu proverb, "Thiga has been initiated, no more mararanja." You challenge those around you to be concise and precise. You possess the attributes that are ascribed to the Great Father. You are the most logical, cohesive, and consistent of all types. You are quicker to observe redundancy, incohesiveness, contradictions, and irrelevancy than other types. You delight in expanding, clarifying and rethinking an idea. You have superior intellectual powers of concentration and comprehension. You, however, appear to other types as arrogant, rude, and an intellectual snob. For that reason, you may be avoided and isolated. It is even worse if you are a female because a woman is not "expected" to be argumentative, critical, or an architect with conceptual originality. You also lack softness of subjectivity, which are attributed to the Great Mother.

With regard to the division of labor, you can be an excellent college and university teacher, logician, mathematician, philosopher, scientist, architect of ideas, or designer. You are of great value to the society since there is only one of your type in every hundred people.

i. ESTP

If you are an ESTP, you might have been labeled as a trouble shooter, a slow learner, hyperactive, or restless; yet, you know (other people also realize) that you are charming, witty, humorous, friendly, attractive, empathetic, pragmatic, realistic, and a practical joker. As with other SPs, you care less about the authority figures. You are better than all types in selling an idea or a project. You have the enormous ability of reading minimal facial expressions.

The above qualities make a good athlete, adventurer, warrior, administrator, negotiator, entrepreneur, diplomat, ambassador, and conflict-manager. You are, indeed, an action-orientated-realist. There are 12 percent of your type in the population.

j. ESFP

If you are a Gikuyu girl, you might be nicknamed Nyaguthii, a traveler, she who is here and there. Whether a male or female, you are likely to be misperceived as egotistical, flighty, and hyperactive. But, for sure, you know that you are clever, talkative, charming, voluble, enthusiastic, exciting, witty, optimistic, concrete, realist, literal, fashionable, and generous. You are, indeed, the most generous of all types. You give without expecting a return. But, sometimes you don't have a clear distinction between what is yours and what belongs to another person. Your philosophy is: "All mine is thine and thine is mine." In addition, you are humane, sensitive, and caring. You have a capability of living in the here and now more than other types. By being optimistic and by having the propensity to enjoy life, you have the lowest tolerance for anxiety.

In your career choice, you ought to avoid a job that will require a rigid routine. You can, however, get great pleasure as a performing artist, public relations officer, airline attendant, social worker, receptionist, primary school teacher, seller of the visible commodity, or in child care, animal husbandry, athletics, and any other job that involves working with people.

k. ENTP

As an ENTP, people will complain that you are unpredictable, whimsical, and inconsistent. Yet, you have strengths that are lacking in other types. You are a motivator, innovative, talkative, optimistic, adaptive, novelist, nonconformist, imaginative, pragmatic, intuitive, ingenious, a conversationalist, an improviser, an inventor, an analyst, and functional. Your contagious humanity magnetizes people to you. You are the best in both intra and interpersonal relationships. You have, nevertheless, a low regard for those in power.

Like your sister, ESFP, you can perform better in a non-routine job, but unlike her, you can tackle innovative, challenging, and complex projects. You can fit into both mechanical and societal professions. You can be an art teacher, master of ceremony, funeral director, entrepreneur, and any undertaking that involves inspiring and motivating people, provided it does not involve a routine. You will find five people of your kind in every hundred people.

l. ENFP

As an ENFP, you have unusual psychic qualities, which enables you to perceive and feel another person's feelings and articulate a person's mannerisms in such a way that you appear as though you are over-identifying with that person. Hence, people may shout at you, "Kamau Kanyi," Kamau's identification or Kimenyi wa Gura, he/she who possesses a piercing knowledge. You may be accused of being hypersensitive, hyperalert. But for sure, you are optimistic, enthusiastic, dynamic, social, affirmative, supportive, gregarious, simultaneous, a motivator, and an inventor of ideas and projects. You are, indeed, a charming, gentle, sympathetic, dramatic, artistic, imaginative, ingenious, and highspirited person. You like to praise others and to be praised by others. You like people more than other types. You like pleasing authority figures—parents, teachers, priests. To most teachers, you are an ideal student.

You can perform well in any job that involves handling people. You can be remarkable theologian, salesman, politician, family physician, teacher, and performing artist. There are only five people of your kind in every hundred people.

m. ESTJ

Even if people complain that you are skeptical, impersonal, and opinionated, you know very well that behind these seemingly weaknesses lies strong qualities. You are, indeed, logical, orderly, detailed, realistic, decisive, a planner, an organizer, a controller, regular, firm-minded, practical, outgoing, and assertive. By being assertive, people know where you stand on any issue. Administration is your birth-right. You have both your primary and secondary groups at heart and you are a pillar of your community. When you are in charge, however, you like surrounding yourself with "yes" people. Besides being an administrator, you can also do well in management, teaching, business, supervisory situations, and in business, law, and church ministry. You can be a loyal marriage partner and an excellent parent. There are 13 percent of your type in the population.

n. ESFJ

There are 13 percent of your type in your village. You tend to bore people with your "shoulds" and "should nots." Being a Feeler, you are soft-hearted, humane, harmonizer, who is warm, trusting, an appreciative. In addition, you are an experimenter, practical, factual, a joker, a realist, conscious, orderly, and a nurturer of institutions, such as church, school, family. You are a remarkable host and a strict but loving parent. Whether male or female, you possess the substance of the Great Mother more than other types. Drawing from this precious substance, you expect people to respect and obey the Great Father.

Professionally, you can be a successful clergy, nurse, receptionist, home economist, salesman, teacher, supervisor, and child psychologist.

o. ENFJ

If you are a Gikuyu ENFJ, you might have heard people referring to you as, Kanua monjore, sweat mouth or soothsayer, or Nyahoro, he-who-wins-people-to-himself-withpersuasive-calmness. You are, for sure, an ideal group leader, collaborator, persuader, motivator, participant, nurturer, and are humorous, caring, concerned, popular, magnanimous, trustworthy, influential, and empathetic. You have a gift of discernment. You intuitively become aware of the climate of the public opinion and you have the audacity of verbalizing the feelings of the community. Martin Luther King, Jr., who was an ENFJ, attracted a large crowd for possessing the spirit of the community and his ability to vocalize this spirit. Until today, thousands of the American people congregate around his spirit once a year. Tom Mboya and Josiah M. Kariuk, the most remarkable Kenyan politicians, were ENFJ.

Professionally, as an ENFJ, you can be a good clergy, performing artist, therapist, teacher, executive, salesman, and leader, particularly social and recreational leadership as opposed to task leadership.

I don't want to scare you by hinting to you that your type tends to attract the assassin's bullet, but Tom Mboya and Josiah M. Kariuk were assassinated for magnetizing all the Kenyans to their spirit, which was Kenya's spirit, thereby, provoking the jealousy of the late Jome Kenyatta. The same thing happened to Martin Luther King. I, therefore, advise you to take care of yourself. But do not fear to die for the community.

p. ENTJ

There are 5 percent of your type in the general population. People murmur that you are rude, arrogant, obnoxious, abrasive. But, you are, indeed, commandant, hearty, competitive, confrontational, an empiricist, robust, objective, competent, and independent. You possess most of the qualities that are attributed to the Great Father. You have exceptional leadership ability. You can do well as managing director, executive director, educational administrator, lawyer, mortgage broker, scientist, planner, and communicator. You can do a superb job in the upper level of management.

D. Division of Labor and Counseling

As we have observed in this chapter, the Gikuyu had a particular cultural heritage, which influenced their division of labor. To be able to understand, and bring understanding to their experiences, counselors need to have some knowledge of their culture. Likewise, every client who comes for counseling has an ethnical heritage, which must be understood and appreciated. The counselor should be aware of the fact that while the client's perception and interpretation of meaning is influenced by over-arching province of meaning of his country, he is also influenced by the symbolic universe of meaning of his particular people. He or she is a part of his village. Individuals and society do not denote separate phenomenon; they are, indeed, simply a collective and distributive aspect of the same. An individual is bound into the whole of which he is a member, and to consider him apart from the whole is quite as artificial as to consider society apart from individuals. As we have seen, the scriptures and African ontology delineates a human person as both and at the same time "I" and "We." Anthropos was created by "Let us"—the deity who manifested himself in oneness. Likewise, the Africans perceive an individual as both one and many. In Professor John Mbiti's words, "I am because we are, and since we are, therefore, I am."

In counseling, we must pay attention to objective psyche by examining the dreams of and studying the literature about our client. We must struggle to understand both primary and secondary groups of the individual's concern. We also ought to understand the blessings and curses of the individual's nuclear and extended family. The individuals never escape from what they have learned at home as children.

In family counseling, we need to find out whether every member of the family is playing his role or whether house chores are left in the hands of the father, mother, or maid. Are children being trained in holding family and communal responsibilities? When should training for work start? It should start in infancy. Indeed, the human should be made aware of and be trained for religious, social, political, and economical duties. Traditionally, the African parent trained the child to reciprocate by giving her the milk then the parent would sip some milk. This is done repeatedly until the child learns to volunteer to feed the mother or father. In the same manner, the mother puts food on the plate and then takes back a small portion.

Gradually, the child learns how to share and to do for others what is done for him.

My wife and I commenced training for religious, political, and communal responsibilities at zero year with our children. We believe the parent should train and facilitate a child to "increase in wisdom and in stature and in favor with God and man." We guided them to wisdom by imparting our morals and ethics, which draw from African and JudeoChristian heritages. We trained them to take care of their bodies, which are the temple of God. We facilitated the growth in "favor with God" by instructing them in the word of God and training them to pray and to be in a worshipping community. They learned how to say their prayers when still in their cribs. We aided them in increasing in "favor with man" by our love of and respect to the people around us. We communicated to them our philosophy of humanity. We believe that while there is evil in the world, humans are fundamentally good. Their goodness is not determined by their color, race, or language. We teach them to be servants of God and human beings.. Mom and Dad, and sister and brother, are a part of these invaluable communities. Thus, our children had to start by performing domestic chores. They started by doing to the parents as the parents did to them. After our toddler, Isaac Cyprian, learned how to bottle feed mom and dad at zero year, he enjoyed washing their faces in the same manner, as they do to him. On one evening, I had a startling experience. I was dozing off on the sofa after a busy day.

I was surprised by Cyprian, with a wet towel on my face. The toddler was wiping my face with a towel, which he had dipped in a toilet bowl. He was doing the best he could for the dad. Since dad wipes his face when it is dirty, he has to wipe his to keep him clean and alert.

As far as the division of labor is concerned, each member of the quartet has a specific role. The two-year-old boy turns off the TV set during the family prayer. He pulls off dad's and mom's shoes and puts them in the closet. Rehema (fifteen) is a dishwasher and assists mom in the laundry and kitchen. Mom is responsible for the kitchen, laundry, and the toddler. Dad is a garbage and yard man. We work in the garden together, buy grocery together, and have family and church worship together.

As far as temperament is concerned, each member makes a unique contribution. Mom, being an ISFJ, helps the family to project the best public image and maintains fundamental values, which we have acquired from our Kenyan-JudeoChristian heritages. She is responsible for details. With her talent of remembering our past, she uses her memory to inspire our today. Our daughter, who is an ESFP, imbues the family with laughs and light-heartedness, reminding us of our anniversaries, birthdays, special days, and the importance of living and enjoying our here and now. While I am the breadwinner, Mary and Rehema are people winners. They are good at making and keeping friends.

Dad, being an INTJ, is responsible for setting the family goals and challenging the family to engage in constant self-improvement. While our varied temperaments are complimentary, they are also sources of our conflicts. For instance, while Mary and Rehema regard a particular success as an end to itself, for me it is a process to the endless end. And, thus, I have the annoying habit of making this comment, "What you have done will help you to become…." To this, sometimes, Mary and Rehema may respond in unison. "To become! Can't you be contented with what I/we have done?" Mary may irritate us with historical citations, particularly, when she uses our past so as to control our present or make us feel guilty. To this, Rehema and dad may shout antiphonically, "We cannot dwell in the past!" Rehema's personality, which is dominated by the "here and now" and "all thine is mine, and mine is thine," may prefer to have a good time first, and then work. Mary and I may shout at her, "Work first!" She may turn this into a joke and say, "If you ever trace your roots you will discover that you are a brother and a sister." She, however, believes that our family is one of the best families in the world. Isaac Cyprian has not yet done his psychological test. But, he is a clown, who enjoys tickling and being tickled. We, of course, enjoy each other immensely, as we move from form to formless, from cosmos to chaos, and structure to antistructure. Our anti or non-structured selves are like the joints that bind us together. It is like our night, which gives us enormous appreciation of our day light.

Thus, while the division of labor expresses our structured self, it is important that we understand that we have a sphere, which is antistructured, irrational, and chaotic. Hence, a complete order is impossible, and for that reason, we have a famous expression, "To err is human; to forgive is divine."

a

CHAPTER NINE

The Antistructure: Mararanja

A. What is Mararanja?

I have mentioned that irua started with mararanja dances, and that during this occasion, people were free to dance the whole night and to sleep away from the houses. I have noted that mararanja was marked with freedom of expression and freedom of being. A person was free to utter whatever was in his mind and to be whatever he liked, provided that he did not harm anyone. A person was free to be as crazy as he liked and whatever he did or said was allowed to go with the wind. Mararanja allowed people to be disorientated and antistructured.

It is my contention that mararanja externalized and ritualized a motif that is inherent not only in the Gikuyu community, but also in all human communities. Indeed, mararanja is that part of us which yearns to be away from the house— the house being an archetype of self. It is our disorientated, antistructured, and chaotic self.

B. Mararanja and the International Community

I have observed mararanja in international gatherings consisting of American, European, and African peoples. The most interesting international mararanja in which I have participated was during the staff institute of the Association of Theological Institutions in Eastern Africa (ATIEA). The gathering included American, German, British, and African religious educators. Mararanja occurred when we were holding a farewell party for one of the members of staff who was nicknamed "Uncle David." The whole party was marked with excessive freedom of expression. We played "the child" and became antistructured. The Bible was read in an awkward and heretical way. The reader started reading from the last word of the last sentence of the last paragraph of the last chapter of the last book of the Old Testament. History was also taught backwards. The whole occasion was marked with a feeling of joy and liberation. Just as the initiates became everything they were not supposed to be during mararanja, we became everything that a good teacher ought not to be.

Furthermore, I witnessed several mararanja when I was studying in the United States. I was astonished to observe mararanja that were very similar to the Gikuyu ones. These ceremonies were cyclical. They occurred during the orientation program for the new students and the last supper for the senior students.

The orientation ceremonies included cookouts, putting on masks, "playing the fool," and excessive freedom of expression. During the farewell party for the senior students, the middle students dramatized the idiosyncrasies of the senior students and faculty members. The mannerisms of the professors and the leaving students were so exaggerated that some professors became angry and decided never to attend senior's farewell parties again.

The integration of the sexes is one of the answers. Let the boys and the girls study together, confront and compete with each other and become familiar with one another and learn how to live together as sexual beings. As was traditional, young men and women who were initiated together, and lived in the same lodge and attended the same school, these students were in an integrated school learning how to live together like an age group. The girls ceased to appear beautiful, but weak angels in the eyes of boys. They became real human beings with their strengths and short comings. They ceased to be mere sexual objects by demonstrating that their psychic energy was equal to that of the boys. On the other hand, the girls will discover that boys are not all powerful protecting angels, but human beings with strengths and weaknesses. They learn the psychology of how to handle the persons of the opposite sex. By sitting together in the class, playing together and rubbing each others' shoulders, they learn how to experience their sexuality without coitus or what the Bible terms as fornication. Christian unions that allow both young men and women to be together, to praise God at the top of their voices, and just become ecstatic can provide an outlet for their irrationality. It is in this respect that Christian unions, and charismatic movements are useful for youths.

The school, college, and university can minimize or even prevent abnormal communal lostness by organizing social evenings, which include students and teachers. This should provide a complete freedom of expression. All should be free to operate through the mararanja sphere. Since mararanja is both non-structured and antistructured, the teachers ought to be vulnerable enough for negative criticism. But whatever is said at this time should be allowed to go with the wind.

In St. Paul's United Theological College, we played our mararanja during social evenings and what we called "teachins" and college fellowships. During the teach-in, all the students and tutors gathered to debate a particular motion. In addition to being rational, one is free to be irrational and express ones' feelings in ones' own way. One is also free to confront. The students confront each other. They also confront the tutors and the college authority. The tutors also enjoy confronting each other and the college authority.

The college fellowship brings the students, tutors and the members of the College Council together. We confront each other. The students and the tutors express their feelings about the members of the College Council—and the authority figures. On the other hand, the members of the council may challenge and confront the students and the tutorial staff. In most cases, the members of the council find it very rough since they do not expect attack and irrational expression from the scholars. Consequently, some of them do not attend the fellowship. One of the council members who decided never to attend the fellowship was reported to have said, "If fellowship means confrontation, I shall never attend it again." However, a good number of the members of the council, allowing themselves to be vulnerable, have continued to attend this annual fellowship. On this occasion, our mararanja is given freedom to express itself. We normally have five hours of mutual confrontation and attack. This is followed by the service of the word of God and Holy Communion. Consequently, the college community is left with great love, peace, and unity. This saves us from abnormal lostness.

In addition, the social evening brings the whole college community together. The program includes concerts, roleplays, jesting, and laughter. The students enjoy the freedom, over exaggerating the traits of teachers and the college authority. This occasion provides an excessive freedom of expression.

This type of get-together, which brings the students, teachers, and administration together, can save the institution from abnormal lostness, such as ceaseless crying, laughing, or strikes that could result in destroying the college ideals. Nevertheless, it has to be born in mind that lostness is a motif that is in both an individual and a community. Thus, at times we have to be mixed up or as we say in Kiswahili, "tutachanganyikiwa." We have, therefore, to go through a period of alienation, precariousness, and disorientation. Yet, this is the time when we must be on our guard since the devil will exploit the state of lostness to take us to captivity. We must pray without ceasing as our Lord Jesus Christ did. We must be in him who is the Way.

As we have seen, we get lost during the rites of passage when we are moving from one developmental stage to another, from one social status to another, from one place to another. We are also affected by the passages of our loved ones. We may become temporarily disoriented during the death of our parent, our child, our brother, or our sister. This lostness, whether normal or abnormal, is not without pain.

a

CHAPTER TEN

The Structure

A. *The Structure and Initiation*

While precircumcision dances gave the initiates an unlimited freedom of expression and of being unstructured, the dances prepared them for the actual day of operation, when they were expected to be totally structured. They were expected to control their feelings, emotions, and bodily expressions. At the peak of pain, they were expected to sit or stand still like stones. We have noted how Mugo Gacheru felt during his highest point of pain. "He (the circumciser) held my penis, pulled the foreskin, and cut it. It was very, very, painful. But I did not show any feeling of fear or even acted as if I were being cut. No medical aid was applied first or later, and this made it extremely painful." Although Gacheru felt a lot of pain, he was expected to sit emotionless. This was a symbolic expression of the life of an initiated person. He was expected to be well behaved and organized. As a Gikuyu proverb put it: "Thiga is circumcised, there is no more mararanja." This means we are not at a mararanja occasion and, therefore, we must be intentional and rational. Whatever one says, he will be accountable for it. Thus, while the initiated person was free to release his sphere, which is mararanja once every year during mararanja and occasionally with his age-group, he was expected to be well mannered, to respect and obey those in authority and to live in accordance with social norms. As we have seen, the Gikuyu community was well organized. Each one knew what to do and what was expected of him; in a given task, each sex knew what to do. Here we can move from particular to universal and argue that structure is found in every human community. All people have norms and laws that govern them. There is no country that has automobiles and no traffic laws. The drivers know whether they have to drive on the right or left sides. So when driving, we are expected to be structured, rational and intentional. Indeed, we are expected to respect and obey the law. The structured sphere in us enables us to do so.

B. *The Structure and Religion*

It is very interesting to note that Paul discusses the structured spheres of human personality within the context of life in the spirit (Roman 7: 12, 14; 1 Corinthians 12-14). He termed this sphere law, order, and mind. He saw it as holy, just, good, and spiritual. He advised the Church to use this sphere in intergroup relations, teaching, preaching, liturgy, and public speech. In these passages, Paul saw the tension between mararanja and the structured self. He admonished his readers to use mararanja in their private prayers or in a group in which all the members have undergone the same experience. However, in their relations with the outsiders, they should be rational, intentional, and structured. "For if the whole church assembles and all speak in tongues, and the outsiders or unbelievers enter, will they not say that you are mad," Paul indicated to his readers that God has given them power to control their mararanja, "For God is not a God of confusion but of peace." He reminds them that "the spirits of prophets are subject to prophets."

In the history of Christian thought, Richard Hooker is one of the thinkers who advocated the structured sphere. Like Paul, he used the term "law" to describe this entity. He put law under two categories: the first law eternal and the second law eternal. Through the first law eternal, God governs himself by his own voluntary act. Under the second law eternal, He governs the natural agents, celestial beings, and national creatures. In other words, for Hooker, rationality or reason is divine, supernatural, rational, scriptural, and human. Of course, Hooker himself lived a very structured life. As one historian wrote, "His voice was law, stature little, gesture none at all, standing stone-still in the pulpit, as if the posture of his body were the emblem of his mind, unmovable in his opinions." Possibly owing to the strong opposition from Puritans who were against the law and structure, Hooker took an extreme position and suppressed his mararanja. However, he reminds us that we cannot live without law and order. As we shall see later, law and order, rationality and intentionality, are some of the attributes of the Great Father.

C. *The Antistructure and Structure*

To this end, it suffices to say that we need to balance between the antistructured self and structured self. We should know where and when to be structured. For instance, we cannot avoid being structured in our daily work, when driving, in the law court, and when we are interacting with strangers. We should have the freedom of living our antistructured self during mararanja (e.g., the eve of All Saints Day, the Feast of the Fools, the ceremonies of separation, social evenings, and when we are with our cliques, age groups, and primary groups. It would also be rewarding if we could have a day once in a while when one can walk at random. At this time, we need to listen to and obey our day dreams and fantasies. This would be a celebration of our mararanja or irrationality. Rank identified the vitality and dynamism of the spheres.

He advised his readers to release and accept them.

The only remedy is an acceptance of the fundamental irrationality of the human being and life in general, an acceptance which means not merely a recognition or even admittance of our basic primitivity in the sophisticated vein of our typical intellectuals, but a real allowance for its dynamic functioning in human behavior, which would not be lifelike without it." For Rank, real life meant expression of both the rational and irrational self. Here one can conclude that if the inner mararanja is totally buried, this results in violence and neurosis. The situation can even worsen during the "passages" and lead to an abnormal lostness.

a

CHAPTER ELEVEN

Lostness

A. *What is Lostness*

The word lostness is used with a notion of temporary confusion, conflict, disorientation, and precariousness, which one undergoes during the rites of passage. It includes the idea of a Swahili word, "kuchanganyikiwa," being mixed up. It also bears the meaning of a Gikuyu word, "Guturura," meaning a temporary blindness, which one experiences when one is dazzled, or lost for a while. A person undergoes lostness when he is confronted with choices. For example, when one is in a situation whereby there are so many open doors, yet one must enter through one of them; or when one hears so many conflicting voices, yet must listen and follow only one of them. So lostness refers to the state of mind before one makes a choice.

As we have seen, the genius of the irua lies in the fact that the entire community celebrated, ritualized, and externalized the inner lostness of adolescence. This ritualization was performed during the mararanja dances when the community became ecstatic, disorientated, and non-structured. It is my thesis that what was externalized during this occasion is a reality that is inherent in every individual and every human community. We undergo a state of temporary confusion or disorientation when we are moving from one developmental stage to another, from one place to another, and from one social status to another. This lostness can be either individual (that is, affecting one person) or communal (that is, affecting a group of people).

B. Communal Lostness

Let me illustrate what I mean by communal lostness. I have just delivered a lecture on the "stages of development from birth to old age" to the Family Life Education, and in-service course for Kenya school teachers held at Limuru Conference Centre. After the delivery, the teachers asked far reaching questions about the problems that are facing the youth. One of these questions was about a communal lostness. The question was: *What is the cause of the recurrent hysteria that sweeps across East African girls' boarding secondary schools?* Normally, this phenomenon sparks from one school and then spreads to other schools. Its nature is that one girl starts laughing or crying then eventually all the girls cry. Gradually, this uncontrollable emotional outburst sweeps across girls' boarding schools in East Africa. In some schools, this lostness is so severe that it results in a temporary closure of the school. Dr. Sebastian K. Lutahoire writes that these were not isolated cases of "examination fever." For instance, sometimes whole schools had to be closed because of mass hysteria, a state of mental disturbance. One of the Christian girls' schools in West Lake Region, Tanzania had to close for this reason for a period of time. 1

In a different form, this communal lostness is evident in our colleges and universities. The students may boycott the lectures, become unruly, and throw stones at passers-by.

This may lead to a temporary closure of the institution.

In Africa, where people unite behind a person rather than a system, the whole county may be left stranded when the head of the state dies or when he is over-thrown. In Kenya, for instance, the whole country was left stranded when the death of the late Mzee Jomo Kenyatta was announced. The majority of the Kenyans were hysterical and did not know what to do and where to go. They were temporarily confused.

More often than not, the church experiences communal lostness when she is moving from one era to another or when she is ushering in a new orthodoxy. She had a real struggle when she was admitting the first generation of gentile Christians. This trend continued in all epochs of the history of the church and will never halt until Christ comes.

The most recent incident that sparked off the debate in the Anglican communion is the election and consecration of Barbara Harris as suffrican bishop of Massachusetts. The consecration was a rite of passage for both Bishop Harris and Catholic Christendom, which claims unbroken apostolic succession of the episcopate. This single event, which took place in Massachusetts, had and will continue to have enormous effect on the Anglican communion and the Roman Catholic and protestant churches.

For the innovators, liberals, and radicals, the inclusion of women in the episcopate was hailed. It was perceived as a glimmer of light and an act of obedience to the creator God who commanded, "Let there be light." In the words of Rev. Paul Washington, the preacher at consecration service, "The light which we see today began its journey before the beginning of time." To most Christians to have a woman bishop was an indication of church growth in equality and inclusiveness. For that very reason, the majority of the people who attended the historic event were hopeful, proud, and happy. While the celebration was a sacred carnival to the innovators, liberals, and radicals, it was a sacrilegious imposture to the traditionalists. They saw it as an insult to the church. It was contrary to the established orthodoxy—the scriptures, tradition, and constitution of the Episcopal Church. Some people in this camp regarded consecration of a woman bishop as a death. One rector symbolized this feeling by holding a requiem mass. He contended, "I just thought that it is good time to pray for the dead and the dying, and that includes the Diocese of Massachusetts."

Ironically, the consecration of a woman bishop was death and life. It marked a death of an era in which the highest order in Christendom was a "man's society." It was also a birth of an era of total inclusion of male and female in all hierarchies of the church. As the presiding bishop rightly put it, it was "a gift to the Catholic Church and a contribution toward a deeper understanding of the holy orders."

The point that I am making is that the church as a body of Christ experienced substantial conflict during her transitional period. This does not mean that the entire body is disoriented. But some members may be confused and secede from the main fellowship.

C. The Positivity and Negativity of Lostness

As I have pointed out, individual lostness may occur when one is moving from one developmental stage to another, such as adolescence, young adulthood, mature adulthood, and old age. This state of mind may be experienced when one attains a particular rank in church or in society. For example, a person may be temporarily confused immediately after being consecrated a bishop. One may experience a similar feeling after achieving a particular academic qualification. I remember how I felt when I received a letter stating that I had fulfilled all the requirements for a doctoral degree. I was so excited and could not do anything for a week. I felt like a new driver who had just passed his driving test and had been so used to driving with a co-driver, but now had to drive alone.

Lostness may lead to either a negative or a positive result. It may, for instance, lead an adolescent to either delinquency, or joining a charismatic group. The lostness of the mid-life may result in divorce, taking a second wife, deserting the family, joining a seminary, going back to school, or to an excessive search for material things. Lostness during retirement may result in destroying that which the person has built, and bitterness against the emerging authority figures. When the man in authority is approaching the retirement age, he may project his retirement to his subordinates and force them to retire. The head of the state, for instance, may imprison or even eliminate the best politicians who are likely to succeed him. Similarly, a bishop who is about to retire may persecute his priests, particularly those who have potentials for episcopate. I know of a bishop, who when he was approaching the extreme age and his retirement, started giving his priests a hard time. He used constant and unrealistic transfers as a punishment. One priest, who had children in school, was given forty-eight hours notice to move to another parish. He waged war with those priests who were possible candidates for succeeding him. He bragged that he was using better strategy than Adolph Hitler, who foolishly fought several countries together and, therefore, lost the battle. The bishop's strategy was to fight one priest at a time.

In the morning and the early afternoon of his life, this bishop was a facilitator and enabler of the priests. He was a model priest whose parish had produced more priests than any other parish in the diocese. Yet in the twilight of his life, he became disoriented. He abandoned all the ideals that he had cherished in the morning. He became, as it were, a sun that was contradicting itself. The sun drew its rays instead of emitting them. Its light and warmth were declining and being extinguished. Said differently, he became a dry well. The valley which had streams of water in the morning had dried up in the late afternoon. The fertile crescent became barren in the autumn of life.

If home and school life have not provided proper guidance, an individual may lose himself, even in the morning of his life, in such a way that he will not come to himself again. The person may be used to taking drugs and become totally addicted to them. He may become a life-long alcoholic. This misguided individual may deviate from social norms and become delinquent, criminal, and irreligious.

On the other hand, the period of lostness may be a time of great learning and personality growth. For instance, a young person who joins a charismatic or revival movement may gain a spirituality, which he will never lose. A middleaged person who goes back to school may attain an immense spiritual and intellectual growth. A person who is led by his lostness to a far country, like the prodigal son, may learn how to appreciate his country and his father's house. Like the prodigal son, I celebrated my mid-life lostness in a far country—America. This for me was a time of enormous learning. Being free from the demons and taboos of my father's house, I had the opportunity to learn a great deal about human nature and life in general. I had the privilege of looking objectively at my country and, therefore, becoming aware of our cultural strengths and weaknesses. I distinguished between that which is uniquely African from that which is human. . Aside from learning how to accept and appreciate people of other cultures, I had a fresh interest in "my father's house." By being bi-cultural, I became more free with others and with myself.

A person who is undergoing lostness should neither be segregated nor excommunicated. He or she needs to be accepted, appreciated, and loved. In counseling, this person needs to be directed to the Great Father, the Great Mother, and the Tree of God. As we shall see later, a healthy personality is that which balances among and draws life from the three archetypes. A male who has a sick masculine component (animus) finds it difficult to face the Great Father. A woman who suppresses her femininity and a man who has an unhealthy feminine component (anima) will have a problem with the Great Mother. A person with a sick religion does not like to approach the Tree of God. (More about this in Chapters Thirteen, Fourteen, and Fifteen.)

D. *The Causes and Treatment of Lostness*

How do we go about the communal confusion? First of all, we need to know the cause of this behavior. Among other things, there are physiological, physiological, social, and religious causes. As we have seen in Chapter Four, physiologically, the adolescents are bothered by the increase of height and weight, by being too short or too tall, by motor awkwardness, by the growth of the primary and secondary sexual organs, and the unevenness of the rate of sexual maturation for both sexes. Psychologically, they go through a turmoil caused by the infantile repressed urges. These feelings are intensified, thus, the previous defenses are no longer adequate, and therefore a sweeping readjustment is required. Psychosocially, the adolescent mind is in a flux. This is a psycho-social stage between child morality and the ethics to be developed by the adult. Socially, they experience tension between home and school norms and the expectation of the peer group. Religiously, adolescents may experience conflict between their parents' teaching and what they learn from the media and their peer group.

If the school authorities and the parents could be aware of the above facts, this could partly solve the problems of an abnormal lostness. They would not do this by segregating the girls from boys and applying rigid puritanical rules.

I was privileged to visit a girls' school a few days after the communal lostness. The school was managed and sponsored by the Roman Catholics. All the teachers in the school were nuns and all the students were girls. No male could enter the school compound without special permission. The girls were not allowed to leave the school without being accompanied by a nun. One of the incidents that triggered the lostness was the case of a girl who broke the regulation and went to the town for shopping without the presence of a female teacher. Coming back in the evening, the girl was expelled from school. Since her home was six hundred kilometers away from the school, the girl had to wander about at night looking for accommodation. Luckily, she managed to find an Anglican priest's family who accommodated her and gave her food. This incident was followed by an outbreak of laughter. All the girls laughed and laughed and nobody was able to halt their laughter. Some of them continued laughing for so long a time that they had to be taken to the hospital.

It is not impossible to discern the cause of this peculiar lostness. Since this type of hysteria does not occur in day secondary schools or boarding schools, which include both sexes, we could deduce that one of the causes is sex segregation. These females are kept away from the males when they need them most. They are asexualized when their sexuality has reached its zenith. They are compelled to repress the libido when all their defense mechanisms are incapable of doing so. This is just like stopping up all the outlets of a cooking pot when the food is boiling, or like preventing a child from disease infection by sealing his nose and mouth so that he may not inhale the polluted air.

Another cause of this lostness could be a contradiction between the teachers' culture that was enforced to the girls and the girls' traditional culture, which dominated their consciousness, personal unconscious, and objective psyche. In school, the students were indoctrinated with missionaries' culture while the home trained them to live and grow like African women. Dr. B. Kagwa did a clinical study of the communal lostness, which occurred in the Christian girls' schools in West Lake Region, Tanzania. He concluded that this phenomenon was caused by the difficult situation for the young people. For at school and churches, they were indoctrinated with new beliefs; at home, they were exposed to traditions. This contrast must be resolved in one way or another. To eliminate the anxiety, one may choose between "going native" or reverting to total westernization. As in these epidemics, one may elect to get sick to escape difficult situations.

This bears a lot of truth about students' conflicts. In school, they are introduced to a maleless community; at home, they live in a community of males and females and are trained to grow as heterosexual human beings. The missionary school segregates them according to their sexes, traditional school is sexually integrated. In school they are taught to believe and adhere to an asexualized deity, at home this deity is irrelevant. So these conflicts put young people into a difficult situation. They become confused.

Another cause of this emotional outbreak is the denial and suppression of the mararanja. As we have seen, this is the human sphere that is anti-structured, non-structured, and irrational. Since this sphere is real, creative, and forceful, it can strongly steam out or dynamically react like a storm if it is totally suppressed. If this happens in school, this dynamic reaction is beyond the control of both the students and the teachers.

How can we save the students, from abnormal communal lostness, which results in either a group hysteria or school strike? How can we allow the spirit to move on this formless and chaotic sphere and therefore continue the creation of order, form, and unity?

a

CHAPTER TWELVE

Pain

A. The Particularity and Universality of Pain

As we have seen, the initiates were expected to confront pain with courage. During the actual operation, which was very painful, they sat or stood still, without showing bodily movement or any emotion. This was an act of ritualization of pain, which is inherent in the human life cycle. Pain is real in every human community. As one writer has said, "Walk slowly for everyone you meet has a cross." Let me illustrate this with an experience from the staff institute of the Association of Theological Institutions of Eastern Africa, which was held in Arusha, Tanzania in April, 1982.

As noted earlier, the Institute included religious educators from Sudan, Uganda, Kenya, Tanzania, and Ethiopia who belonged to Roman Catholic, Anglican, and Protestant Churches. Being drawn from several African states, the United States of America, and European countries, the members belonged to various political ideologies. In addition, they had differing theological convictions since they operated from various theological models. This of course included orthodox, neo-orthodox liberal, radical, and revisionistic models. The theme of the Arusha Institute was "Pre-Christian theologies and their implication in Christian theologies."

The topics dealt with included "Concepts of Revelation in Christianity," "Concepts of God in Africa," "Concepts of God in Christianity," "Concepts of Salvation in Africa," "Concepts of Salvation and Christianity," "Religion and Society in Africa," and "Religion and Society in Christianity." The papers dealing with each of the above topics were presented. All the papers, according to my assessment, were of the highest theological and philosophical qualities. Every presenter had done his "homework." However, each of the presentations was followed by strong arguments and disagreement. The issue was whether or not African traditional religions had full and complete salvation. Dr. Kibicho argued strongly for the full and complete saving power within African religions. This hypothesis bothered the missionaries.

The missionaries' bitter feelings toward African traditional religion were expressed by a question that was directed to Dr. Kibicho by a white teacher: "If African religion had a full and complete salvation, why did you become a Christian minister rather than a witch doctor?"

After the presentation of all the papers, the writer had to organize a forum. The majority of the participants who were put on the panel were introverted, and had no chance of saying a word for three days. The procedure was that those on the panel had to start by saying something about themselves. After this, everyone was free to ask a question, make a statement, confession, or give a testimony.

To the writer's surprise, every person started sharing his pain. Arguments and disagreements halted. Behind highquality philosophical and theological papers there was found a common ground - suffering and pain. In the majority of the states that were presented, Christians had and were still being persecuted. Thus, in pain and suffering, we were all united and had a feeling for each other. Pain is a reality. Pain is universal. C. S. Lewis rightly contend that The possibility of pain is inherent in the very existence of a world where souls can meet.

Pain may be a spiritual or mental distress—a bodily torment or a distressing sensation in a particular part of the body. Physical pain may be caused by an accident, sickness, or some chemical problems in the body. Spiritual pain may be caused by sin or keeping aloof from the religious community. Chemical disorder, an unpleasant environment, movement from one place to another and from one developmental stage to another, the attainment of anew social status, and bereavement can bring mental suffering. As Raymond Schmitt observed the amount of mental pain experienced may in part depend on the distance between one's actual state and one's ideal state. That is a gap between what one actually is and what one wishes to be.

Mental pain can be caused by a discrepancy between what a person thinks he can become and what he can actually become. For instance, one may wish to be a musician while having no potential for music.

B. Pain and Religion

As we have seen, pain is one of the motifs in the passages of Christ. First of all, he was born in a manger. Moreover, when he was twelve, he went with his parents to Jerusalem. His parents lost him in the temple and it must have pained them to lose him for three days. Before starting his ministry, he was led by the Holy Spirit to the wilderness where he was tempted by the devil; he was hungry and thirsty. Finally, he was rejected by his own people —the chief priests, the scribes, and the elders. Consequently, he went through the agony of the cross. He was killed and buried in tomb. On the third day, God raised him from the dead and "highly exalted Him, and bestowed on him the name which is above every name" (Philippians 2:9).

Jesus understood very well that pain was a part of his life and that it was the divine plan for him to suffer. Pain and suffering was a part of his service to man and God, "for the son of man also came not to be served but to serve, and to give his life as a ransom for many" (Mark 10:45).

Paul understood Christian suffering as a participation in and identification with Christ. "If we have died with Christ, we believe that we are also to live with him" (Roman 6: 5, 8). It is only by accepting the pain of the cross that a Christian will be glorified and exalted with and in Christ. For Paul, life was a struggle and victory, death and resurrection. Pain, therefore, is not a hypothesis but a reality. It can have a positive or a negative effect. It may lead to inappropriate anger, guilt, depression, or withdrawal. If a person loses a loved one, he may be bitterly angry with God or other people. He may feel guilt for not doing what he was "supposed to do." He may have a prolonged aloneness, which may lead to an extreme loneliness. He may condemn someone who is suspected to have caused the death. The bereaved may seek comfort from drugs and become alcoholic or drug addicted.

C. Pain and Personality Growth

Erik H. Erikson theorized that the pain that a person experiences during maturational stages may have a permanent negative effect on his personality. A child who lacks a reliable and dependable mother may develop basic mistrust and consequently develop the most dangerous defense mechanism—introjection and projection. In introjection, he makes other people's pain and "garbage" his own; in projection he throws his undesirable qualities and inner hurt to others. He blames others for his own evil. If the child is over-controlled, he may develop shame and doubt. Subsequently, he may become a person who tries to force the world not to look at him and to destroy the eyes of the whole world. He may blame things and regard them as evil only because they exist. He may also develop guilt and inferiority feelings. He may be feeling guilt for what he is and feel inadequate in the presence of his tool partners. He may suffer from ego-diffusion. In adulthood, one may suffer from self-absorption, stagnation, and despair. In old days in the Gikuyu community, if a person became stagnant, despairing, and totally withdrawn from the community, he was burned alive in his own house. Thus, pain may block the road to integrity and can be destructive to oneself and to others.

On the other hand, pain can help an individual to attain intimacy and integrity.

Gikuyu and other African people realize that pain can make a positive contribution to one's maturation and prosperity. This is expressed by numerous expressions and proverbs. Gikuyu for instance has a proverb, which says, "Pain cannot be felt by one for the other" (Ruo rutiguanagirwo). This means that it is through suffering that one becomes an individual and attains self identity. In Kiswahili, we say, "subira ya vuta heri" (patience evokes or brings blessing). This implies that it is by accepting suffering that one receives blessings from others, and being blessed, one can also bless. Ironically, acceptance of pain and suffering is seen by African people, as the key to comfort and prosperity. Our parents and teachers tell us, "Subira ni ufunguo wa faraji," (patience is the key to comfort). We are advised, "Fuata nyuki ule asali," (follow bees and get honey). It is only by accepting the sting of the bees that you can get honey. The African believes that tribulation is followed by comfort and prosperity. It is maintained that a good omen lies beyond the obstacles, "Munyaka wi mbere ya kahinga. "

According to Erik Erikson, if the child is well guided during maturational pain, he attains basic trust, autonomy, initiative, industry, and self-identity. Subsequently, when he matures, he gains intimacy, generativity, and integrity. For Erikson, integrity is the ultimate goal of a well-adjusted personality. The person who attains this goal is one who has taken care of things and people, and has adapted himself to triumphs and disappointments (pain)—someone who has been the originator of others or the generator of products and ideas. This view is at the heart of the African understanding of personality. It is maintained that integrity is the summit of personality. The individual who attains it is one who has contributed to and drawn from the community. This is expressed by proverbs such as, "muria wiki akuaga wiki," meaning, "He who eats alone dies alone" and "mugi ni mutare meaning," meaning, "To be wise is to accept to be advised by others."

Gikuyu see a connection between wisdom and pain. One of the terms used for initiation is "The wisdom of Gikuyu." To undergo the pains and ordeals of initiation is regarded as a means of assimilating the whole gamut of tradition, norms, custom, values, and wisdom of the tribe.

D. Pain and Philosophy

Existential philosophers, like the traditional men maintained that painful experiences can lead to wisdom. They witnessed a direct connection between suffering and wisdom. Their perception was influenced by the anguish, which pervaded their epoch—the horror of the two world wars, which destroyed national, regional, and cosmic centers; political and religious totalitarianism, revolutions and terrorism, slave trade, and apartheid; and spiritual bankruptcy, caused by materialism and worship of science and technology. There were also agonizing conflicts between democracy and dictatorship, individualism versus collectivism, colonization versus decolonization, freedom of thought or anti-intellectualism, and pluralistic society or absolute values and conformity. People of this era lived in tension between suppression or expression, reformation, or conformation.

Thus, influenced by their daily experiences and observations, the existentialists asserted that humans lived in distress caused by fear of nothingness and alienation. They observed that anguish is the underlying, all pervasive, universal condition of human nature. Humans live in a stormy world that is devoid of peace. They are thrown into the world against their will. As Sorem Kierkegaard lamented, "Who am I? How did I come into the world? Why was I not consulted?" Kierkegaard perceived himself as a creature who was thrown into the world against his will. He was thrown here to be there for a short duration only to be soon swallowed up in the eternity. While he was in this temporal life, he occupied a minute space and was ignorant of the rest of the universe. This situation caused mental and physical strains.

In addition, existentialists asserted that renaissance philosophers contributed to human suffering by alienating the humans from the absolute. They killed the ideal JudeoChristian God by their empiricism, which overstressed empirical verification. This was in direct opposition to Christian principles, which advocated: "We go by faith, not by sight." By loss of belief in God, humans have lost the foundation of their truth and values.

Thus, the humans are agonized by being alienated from their traditional values and their social systems and, thereby, live lives of vanity and meaninglessness. They are estranged from the product of their labor and their religious and political systems. I witnessed this estrangement when I was a theological student at St. Paul's United Theological College. As a part of our theological studies, we had to take urban mission, which among other things, entailed spending two weeks in a factory. I was assigned to work at a textile factory in Thika. We had to stand beside the feelingless machine and operate and feed it for eight hours. The blow-room was poorly maintained and for that reason we had to inhale a lot of cotton dust. Being allergic to dust, I had a terrible cough by the end of the two weeks.

The workers who mistook me for a member of the government's special branch (plain clothed police officer), sent by the government to probe the company, shared all their problems with bitterness. One man narrated his predicament, "I left my wife and children in the countryside two years ago. Never have I gone back since. For after paying all my bills I have no money left to take to my wife. Half of my income pays the rent. A quarter is spent on my poor diet. The other portion goes to a prostitute who washes and massages my exhausted feet and soothes me to give me the comfort I need. I do not know how I will provide for my family. I am worried about them and about my old age." This worker was articulating an anguish experienced by many workers in many countries who are alienated from their families— the product of their labor, their political, social, and religious institutions.

Existentialists assert that human suffering is exasperated by the structurelessness of life. Humans live without anything to structure their beings and their world. They hover at the abyss in fear and trembling. Thrown into nothingness, they move into nothingness and will end up into nothingness—which is death. This final nothingness terminates an individual as a conscious being.

It should be borne in mind that human history, like the Gikuyu life cycle is characterized by passages. These passages, according to culture-epoch theory have three phases: periods of balance, periods of chaos, and periods of adjustment. The period of balance is marked with harmony in basic institutions such as family, school, cult, and politics. Life is very satisfying particularly in the early stage of balance. Eventually, people get bored by the balance. And the new thinkers, artists, and scientists upset the balance and usher in a period of chaos.

In the period of chaos, people find themselves in the wilderness or limbo. This is analogous to mararanja in Gikuyu initiation, whereby nothing is structured. Traditional values do not hold. There are wars and civil strife. While some people strive for new balance, others will try to back the clock to a better and more peaceful "Egypt." Gradually, new discoveries and ideals are accepted. These new attitudes usher in the period of adjustment, whereby people change to conform to the new realities.

Existential philosophy was born out of the period of chaos of human civilization. It was endeavoring to give meaning to human suffering. Existentialists were asking a simple question: "What is it?" The immediate answer was, "It is painful." They then posed other questions. *What is the effect of pain on humans? What can we learn from pain?*

Some of these great thinkers discovered that there is connection between pain and moral and religious growth. Sorem Kierkegaard, for instance, observed that there are three stages of moral development: the aesthetic stage, ethical stage, and religious stage. The aesthetic stage, which is the lowest stage, is characterized by pure sensation and a life of feeling rather than thinking. People who are in this stage live in anonymity. They move with the crowd and are, as it were, in the midway of a carnival being attracted by many games and exhibits. As Plato observed, this stage is lowest in the level of understanding of reality. Persons in this stage can only know the images, reflections, and shadows rather than the real objects. They live in illusion. They are like prisoners chained in the cave, facing the opposite direction of the entrance of the cave. These prisoners can only see the shadow of the real objects.

An individual moves from aesthetical to the ethical stage after a shocking experience such as an accident, serious illness, or loss of a loved one. The highest stage, which Kierkegaard terms a leap of faith or religious stage, is not only attained through painful experiences, but it also leads to greater pain and anguish. This stage is attained by a few. The best example is Abraham, who had to experience the pain of childlessness. And then when he got Isaac, the only son, whom he had yet to sacrifice. He had to murder his own son in obedience to God. As we have seen, it was ordeals and pain that the initiates experienced that made them adults. At the same token, the same pain qualified their parents to be the members of the jury.

Thus, pain, if taken positively can lead to maturity. It can set us free. And like freed prisoners, we can move from the cave to enjoy fresh air, sunshine, and beauty of creation, as well as facing the thunderstorms and hurricanes of life. We experience greater pleasure and greater pain. We discover that there is more to the cosmos than the shadows and images which we have been accustomed to in the cave. We become conscious of universal, spiritual essences. We become cognizant of dialectical realities. We accept the ambiguity of life. We become self transcendent.

Jean Paul Sartre, the father of existentialism, asserted that there is a relationship between anguish and philosophy. He contended that the consciousness of nothingness is the basis of scientific and philosophic inquiry. For Sartre, a human being is a conscious being who is made conscious by the external objects. He is a "being for-itself" which is activated by the being in-itself (all external objects, which includes other humans). Being for-itself (I, as opposed to all external objects and other humans) is empty, nothing, and transparent. There is a gap between being for-itself and being in-itself.

As conscious beings, we are agonized for being cognizant of our freedom. . We dread the awareness of the fact that we are undetermined and, thus, spontaneous, and we have the power of putting a gap between our present and the past. We can make new choices, which are free, and yet it pains us to know that we are responsible for our choices. We are responsible for our perceptions and the meanings that we give to the situations in which we live. Thus, for Sartre, we have a shattering awareness that by being totally free we are also are totally responsible for our choices. This freedom brings dizziness and anguish. Anguish is therefore the outcome of freedom. For Sartre, freedom is neither a gift nor a choice. We are condemned to be free. The limit to freedom is freedom itself. We are not free to cease to be free; hence, we cannot escape from anguish which results from freedom.

On the one hand, I agree with Sartre that I am free to make choices and that I am responsible for my choices. There is also a connection between freedom and pain. As I write this chapter, my son who is eleven months has gone through two infantile developmental stages— teething and walking. Each of these stages is a movement to freedom—teething leads to freedom of chewing solid food. Yet whenever each tooth was appearing, he had a lot of discomfort. At one time, he cried one full hour. The crying was halted after smearing his gums with teething gel. After having upper and lower teeth he has acquired greater freedom of chewing, yet this freedom led to suffering since he was chewing anything that he could lay his hands on. He also had to experience pain related to the freedom of walking. In his first week of walking, he constantly hurt himself as he fell on objects that were in his way.

Thus, it is evident that freedom comes with pain and leads to pain. But on the other hand, existentialists have overstressed human suffering. Since their philosophy is a philosophy without God, they never realized the positive and salvavic aspect of suffering. One of the greatest blessings of being a Christian is that a Christian experiences grace in suffering. In Paul's words, "We rejoice in our sufferings, knowing that suffering produces endurance, and endurance produces character, and character produces hope, and hope does not disappoint us, because God's love has been poured into our heart through the Holy Spirit which has been given to us" (Roman 5:3-5).

The Existentialists have missed the boat by ignoring the Being-who-let-it-be and the Being who is the ground of our being. Furthermore, their philosophy of freedom is one-legged, in that they thought that an individual could be totally free from communality. As we have seen, humans are born as "I" and "we." We are created with a capacity of being "I-ness" and "We-ness." An individual with real and healthy freedom is one who endeavors to balance between individuality and communality.

Killing of the Great Father is another weak point of existential philosophy. Sartre, for instance, never forgave his father for dying when he (Sartre) was an infant or his grandfather, Charles Schwietzer, for mistreating his mother. Sartre's autobiography is a biting, aggressive attack on his parents and grandparents. Not only was he aggressive to his father and grandfather, but he also hated his childhood. He said, "I hated my childhood and everything that remained from it." Owing to the hatred he felt for his roots, Sartre endeavored to formulate a philosophical system that created a gap between himself and his roots. I suggest that no one can ever succeed in putting a void between the human family and the Great Father without destroying the structure. Existence without the Great Father is devoid of rules and regulations that govern the human family. Without the Great Father, we are without ethics and morals. Interestingly, Sartre offered only two laws, which are contradictory in terms—authenticity and inauthenticity. Inauthenticity is a bad faith. It is self deception—deceiving yourself that you are not free to make choices. Authenticity is an acknowledgement that I alone freely choose what I do and I alone am responsible for the consequences of my choices. This philosophy tends to lead to antinomianism. Antinomianism leads to anarchy. Anarchy ushers in human suffering.

Nevertheless I agree with Sartre that pain can be a means to wisdom and freedom. As we have seen, the ordeals that an individual experienced during circumcision gave him a greater freedom—freedom of being an adult and a part of his age group and of learning all the secrets of the tribe. For a Gikuyu, passing through Gikuyu wisdom and instruction, which were attained during the initiation, was not a matter of choice. One was condemned to initiation to tribal wisdom. The wisdom was acquired through suffering in total silence on circumcision day and utter submission to the sponsors during the ordeals of seclusion period.

The suffering was intended to produce an individual who could think philosophically, who was guided by reason rather than feelings, who does not act impulsively on the first feeling he experiences in response to a situation, but who examines that situation from different perspectives. This person, who is initiated into Gikuyu philosophy, was usually guided not so much by passions of the moment, although he may take them into account, but by realities of the situation, the goal he is pursuing, and the principles and values that he found trustworthy. He does not chronically deny his emotions, but does not precipitously give in to them.

The wise person does not totally desert the cave, but unlike other chained prisoners, he broke the chain and had courage to moving outside of the cave so as to face the pleasure of sunshine and beauty of the world as well as the pains of storms, hurricanes, and earthquakes of life. He was far from being narcissistic. He did not have extreme self-love and excessive preoccupation with himself and his own concerns. He made fewer demands on others to satisfy his own pride and wishes. He avoided causing needless suffering to others and to himself also.

Pain, if taken as an initiation, bears positive fruits. It can be redemptive to the sufferers and others. The cross, which is the most significant symbol of the Christian, narrates the story of God who suffered in order to redeem the whole world. The cross is a symbol of God's love— "God shows his love to us for while we were yet sinners Christ died for us."

Thus, in counseling and therapy, we need to be aware of the positive as well as negative aspects of pain. As Josef Goldbrunner observes, "While a pastor should know joy, he must know pain as well, for pain is the element of our salvation-situation. More exactly it is the element most impressive and palpable to man and consequently seems to be predominant in pastoral care."

More often than not, people go to pastors and therapists because of pain. The great temptation of the healing team is to shorten the liminality of life in order to reduce the pain.

We should, however, ask the following questions: *How can I facilitate learning and growth? How can I enable the sufferer to find himself in the wilderness? How can I illuminate the hurting person so that he may find God in the marginal entity? How can the painful situation lead to self examination and self determination? How can the present pain facilitate moral and ethical growth? How can the anguish led the sufferer to maturity and wisdom?*

E. Pain and Treatment

However, the pastors and counselors who work with the Gikuyu (and possibly other African communities who undergo similar initiation rites) need to know that there are some Gikuyu who, because of irua philosophy, tend to idolize pain. They strongly believe that it is only the bitter medicine that heals. They are dominated by the Gikuyu proverb, "Nothing good that comes from a good place" (Gutiri Kiega Kiuma hega). In medical treatment, they may prefer an injection to a capsule. In extreme cases they may reduce the present life to pain and suffering in the hope of getting the brightest future. A Gikuyu may also accept to suffer unnecessary pain. Mugo Gatheru, a Gikuyu student at an American College experienced unnecessary pain when he dated an American girl who had an artificial plate of front teeth. During kissing, Gatheru put his tongue in the girl's mouth. Since her gum did not have sensation, her teeth fell on his tongue. In Gatheru's words: "I felt pain since she was actually biting me and it was exceedingly painful…but outwardly I made it appear as if I was enjoying it. In the end, the kissing was over! I excused myself to go to the lavatory to spit some blood from my tongue."

The reader cannot fail to see a parallel between Mugo's attitude to the kissing session and his attitude to the knife, which cut him during the circumcision. Although the kissing was exceedingly painful, he did not show any feeling of pain. He made it appear as though he was enjoying it. He behaved the same way during the pain of the knife: "It was very, very painful," he says, "but I did not show any feeling of fear or even act as if I were being cut." Mugo being unconsciously influenced by the irua experience, accepted unnecessary pain. What Gatheru did is typical of many Gikuyu. For this reason, when giving pastoral care and counseling to those who are suffering, the priest should try to find out whether or not the suffering is worthy.

It also has to be pointed out that a Gikuyu regards tears as a sign of fear, rejection of pain, and a denial of circumcision. For this reason, most Gikuyu (and other African people) do not understand the positivity of tears in releasing emotional tension. Unfortunately, some bereaved Gikuyu suffer from what psychiatrists term "hypochondria," an abnormal condition characterized by a depressed emotional state. As we have noted, in old days, the Gikuyu bereaved persons released their emotions through sexual intercourse. The widows employed "sword sellers" who slept with them and had sexual intercourse twice a night. Subsequently, these sword sellers became their life-long sexual partners. Interestingly, this custom is still in the deep structure of the Gikuyu mind. A few weeks ago, some Gikuyu friends and I were discussing modern Gikuyu funerals. One of my friends expressed his surprising experience during the wake. "I visited the bereaved at night," he said. "I found many people in the house. Other people were in the yard. After staying in the house for a while I went out to see what was happening. I was astonished to see men and women lying on the grass making love." Dominated by that part of them, which is ancestral, which goes back thousands of years (C.G. Jung terms this realm of personality "Objective Psyche"), the Gikuyu may use sexuality to release their emotion during bereavement. However, they find themselves in tension between their past, which is still in them, and the Christian ethic that condemns any sexual affair outside marriage. The church should give alternative means of releasing the emotion; we need to tell them that tears are one of the most valuable things that God has given us. It purges our psyche and releases our sorrow.

As we have noted, during the circumcision, one is not expected to show any feeling of fear. Gatheru told us how he bravely sat down and folded his fists as a boxer. He also told us about his awareness of the expectation of the crowd, "The crowd was very silent," he says, "waiting perhaps to detect whether I would show a sense of feeling of fear." As Gatheru indicated, a Gikuyu fears his fear. He may fear that his fear will be detected. A circumcised Gikuyu equates the showing of fear with de-circumcision. The priest and counselors need to help the Gikuyu to get in touch with their fear. Fear is a part of human nature. Each person has a particular person, or place or object that can evoke his fear. It is spiritually and psychologically healthy to know the objects that evoke ones fear and to acknowledge them. My own philosophy, which is too costly to be sold to other people, is this: I look at my fear, talk to it, and love it. I pay attention to the places, persons, and things that trigger my fear and admire them. This philosophy has helped me to turn my fear into a friend. I love my fear because it has saved me from being a giant or a super man who cannot empathize with other people.

In conclusion, we have seen that pain may have physical, spiritual, and psychological causes.It may bear negative results; namely mistrust, doubt, shame, guilt, ego-diffusion, inferiority feeling, self-absorption, stagnation, despair, withdrawal, insanity, and death. It can also have a positive effect such as trust, autonomy, industry, identity, intimacy, generativity, integrity, joy, and exaltation. It was the Gikuyu's positive attitude toward pain that encouraged them to suffer and die for their soil and their faith in Jesus Christ in the 1950s. Joy and pain are interwoven in our earthly pilgrimage. Pain is real! The events of pain have a course, like the biological aging process, that continuously influences man...and its movement can be rendered fruitful through a conscious acceptance and formation.

Pain may lead us to the Tree of God, the Great Mother, and to our Father's house.

a

CHAPTER THIRTEEN

The Tree of God

A. Definition of the Term

As we have noted, the name Gikuyu derives from Mukuyu tree. This is due to the fact that, according to our myth, Gikuyu, the father of the tribe, emerged from the roots of the fig tree. Thus, the genesis of the Gikuyu people is associated with the tree. This tree will be termed the Tree of God.

As we have mentioned, the liminal entity included the rite under the tree whereby the senior adviser took beer and poured it around the tree, took some honey and smeared it onto it, and then prayed to Murungu, the ancestral God. He then took the milk juice from the tree and marked the male initiates on their cheeks, around the eyes, the center of their foreheads, hands, and legs. Then the wife of the senior adviser put the milk juice on both of the girls' temples, on their necks, on their nipples, and their hands. Symbolically, this rite connected the initiates with the Tree of God out of which Gikuyu, the founder of the tribe came. Under the Tree of God, they were attached to the mystical sacred time when the Supreme Being was present on earth and mystically revealed himself, in human form, to the father of the tribe. They were also conjoined with Ngai, the Supreme Being and the great Provider, with other mystical beings, the ancestors and the cosmos.

Thus, the term Tree of God will be used to denote that which is in our inner world, which connects us with our primordial time, the Supreme Being, the mystical beings, the ancestors and the mysteries around us. We will also use it for the external phenomenon, objects, insects, and animals that make us aware of this inner reality.

The Tree of God is located in man's "Garden of Eden." It comprises "the tree of the knowledge of good and evil" and "the tree of life," which sustains the human soul. It is the object and subject of people's myths, legends, sagas, proverbs, and idioms. It is the meeting point of anthropos (humanity) and the shekinah (the dwelling of God with his own). Under the Tree of God, we are made aware of the totality of our humanity and the presence of the God, who is the possessor of brightness and who-shines-in Holiness. It also makes us aware of the totality of our environment and our awareness of being and the complexity and the ambiguity of life. Like the ark of the covenant, the Tree of God has both healing and destructive powers (herem).

B. The Communal Tree

We have noted that there is an object that makes an individual aware of the Tree of God. This we shall term an individual tree. In addition, there is an object that makes a particular community aware of the Tree of God. This we shall term the communal tree. For the Gikuyu, the communal tree was the sacred tree which was set apart for Ngai known as muti wa Ngai (the Tree of God). Under this tree, God was worshipped. The tree itself was never worshipped, but it was regarded as sacred and one would not have dared to cut its branches or twigs—or approach it alone at night.

The Gikuyu people project their inner Tree of God to a chameleon, which they revere and fear more than a totem. Let me illustrate. On one occasion, I put a chameleon in a box, covered it with a lid, and took the reptile to a class that consisted of Gikuyu students and students from other ethnic groups. I told the students that I had something in the box that I would take around and that I would uncover the lid as I approached each student. I instructed the students should touch what was in the box without informing other students what they had seen and touched. Interestingly, students from other ethnic groups touched the creature without showing any change of facial expression. But whenever a Gikuyu student saw the animal, he/she was moved to a great sensation of awe. They expressed a sensation similar to that of Adam and Eve when they heard the sound of the Lord God walking in the garden in the cool of the day after they had eaten the forbidden fruit.

After the exhibition, I asked the Gikuyu students to talk about the chameleon. One of the students narrated, "Once upon a time, when God created human beings he told the chameleon, 'Go and tell people, thou shall never die!' As God was talking to the chameleon, the lizard overheard and outran the slow walking reptile to reach the people first and gave them the message of death. The lizard told the people, 'God has said, thou shall surely die and perish.' This is why we die," concluded the student.

After the class, I spent hours with the chameleon in my backyard. I studied its behavior and discovered that it is both swift and slow. Even though it approached the environment stealthily, whenever it saw a prey, its long tongue moved as fast as a bullet. It never missed an insect. It changes its colors not only to conceal itself from the enemy, but also to remain incognito in the presence of the prey. I discovered that the chameleon is one of the most intuitive animals that God has created.

As with the chameleon, the Gikuyu people are extremely intuitive and adaptable. In their search for economic freedom, they possess almost selfless dedication. They have propensity for compromise whenever they perceive that they will benefit from a situation.

Thus, the chameleon is a creature that makes the Gikuyu people conscious of their ontology, their genesis, the origin of life and death, the anthromorphic God who appeared to their forefathers and mothers, and the ambiguity of life. Put differently, the chameleon mirrors the Gikuyu's psychic archetype that I term as the Tree of God.

For many people of the world, a priest or a Shaman is an outward object on which they project their inner Tree of God. The priest, as a mana person, represents powers, which can uproot, pull down, destroy, and overthrow. These powers are also capable of building, planting, nurturing, and sustaining. The mana person symbolizes healing and destructive powers. As a therapeutic symbol, the priest is the means of grace. As a negative symbol, the priest represents herem, which can throw people to the darkness of God in order to usher them into the glorious light of the Deity-who-shines-in-holiness. He mirrors people's morals and makes them conscious of their moral strength as well as their short-comings. The priest may provoke a dreadful feeling or fear of the Holy, just as a chameleon makes the Gikuyu aware of the ancestral God. When I was a teenager we had a parish priest known as Peter Owit, whom we nicknamed "Peter the Rock." Physically, Peter the Rock was a huge man. In addition, the Rock had enormous spiritual energy. His physical and spiritual energy compelled him to move like a lion. One day Peter the Rock, in his priestly collar, paid a surprise visit to the biggest beer hall in town. He dashed in and found hundreds of people drinking beer. Seeing a priest, some people were confounded with awe, threw their mugs of beer on the floor, and ran away. The presence of Peter the Rock evoked the same feeling as the chameleon evoked to the Gikuyu students.

The late professor Urban T. Holmes, III, an American priest who was my teacher and supervisor of my doctoral dissertation, reported an incident, which was similar to that of Peter the Rock. Dr. Holmes, when he was a chaplain in the university, visited students in their dormitory and found them drinking beer. When a student saw the priest, he gasped, "Oh my God!" whirled around, and leapt out of the window.

The two illustrations indicate how the priests from two different cultures and hemispheres elicited the similar feeling. They evoked a feeling of awe, just as the chameleon does to the Gikuyu people. It suffices, therefore, to conclude that priests, rabbis, shaman, and other religious specialists are external objects on which the communities mirror their inner Tree of God.

Other external communal Trees of God include shrines such as church buildings, temples, mosques, and tribal sacred objects, such as sacred mountains, trees, stones, animals, and rivers.

There are also cosmic central Trees of God, which are centripetal for peoples of many cultures, languages, tribes, nationalities, and continents. These cosmic communal trees of God are golden threads, which bind all people together. They give our inner tree of God, which is at the center of our garden of Eden, a feeling of wholeness. For the Roman Catholic, Rome and the Pope are the cosmic central Trees of God. The Anglican Communion has Canterbury and the Archbishop of Canterbury, Jerusalem is the cosmic central Tree of God for all Christians. The Muslims have Mecca as their central tree of God.

The above holy places and persons are centripetal, which magnetizes the human families to the cosmic center. They redeem them from centrifugal forces, which pull them away from the axis. They are indeed analogous to the psychic archetype of the Tree of God, which is located in the center of humankind's garden of Eden.

C. The Individual Trees

The external individual trees may be as many as there are individuals. My own individual tree is a mole. For me, this creature is more than an animal. Its very presence touches my collective unconscious. Our daughter's individual tree is a dog. My wife and I became aware of this when she was three and a half and started developing an awareness of the presence of dogs. She was particularly scared by black furry dogs. When this happened, we remembered how she first found a black dog in my study room when she was two and a half years old. On that occasion she was not scared, but remembered the dog for many years.

At the age of four, she developed a great fear of dogs. Unfortunately, we were living at Sewanee, Tennessee where there were almost as many dogs as there were people. One could not walk for five minutes without meeting a dog. This meant that Rehema had to scream several times a day. This scared us since we were the only African family in that area and Rehema was the only black child in kindergarten. Since her school was also peopled with dogs, she screamed constantly and scared other children and the teachers. While her fear for the dog was becoming greater, my wife and I tried hard to reconcile her with the dogs. I took her to the dog, which she first met in my study room. I had given her a warning in good time so she did not cry when we found the dog. In its presence, I started telling a story.

"Once upon a time there was an African girl living at Sewanee. On one occasion she entered her daddy's study room and saw a dog."

"That girl is me," she interrupted.

"And this is the dog. It is not as black as you. It is as black as me." From this dialogue I learned that there was a real connection between her blackness and the dog, her African root and this totem. As a result of this awareness,

Mary and I decided to have a black girl as Rehema's baby sitter. We got Linda, a disabled girl who was as black as Rehema. So we had to take Rehema to Linda's home. To our surprise, when she saw the black faces of Linda's family, she screamed in the same way as she did in the presence of the dogs. However, we forced her to be looked after by Linda, and after six weeks she stopped crying. Linda and her family became her friends. Interestingly, this lessened her fear of dogs. In further attempts to reconcile Rehema with her individual tree, Mary took her picture when she was in the nude. But when she saw her photograph for the first time, she demonstrated the same feeling as she had for the dogs. After this, we got a black furry dog for her. For seven weeks, she either worshipped the dog or screamed at it. During the seventh week she said she did not want the dog because it was scaring her. Instead of accepting her request, Mary locked her and the dog in her bedroom. Rehema cried and cried until she was tired and then slept. She spent that night with her puppy. This incident not only ended her screaming at dogs, she also developed a positive attitude toward her African roots. She started saying to her American friends: "I am an African girl." And whenever we met a dog, she said, "I don't fear you anymore. You are my friends." However, for her, dogs are more than animals.

At the age of six and a half years, she told us about her creation myth. She narrated: "In the beginning, God created dogs, then the light, and then the trees. And finally he created people." The dogs seem to connect her with the mystical and primordial time.

While the above illustrations clarify my point about external communal and individual trees, they have almost over simplified the meaning of the tree. The external trees are symbols. Symbols are not signs. Symbols emerge from and reach the unconscious. They reveal the unknown and unknowable. While signs speak to the intellect, symbols capture the whole person.

As we have seen, Gikuyu, the father, the founder and the hero of the tribe, emerged from the tree. He was born out of the tree. Thus, the tree is also a symbol of the Great Mother.

C.G. Jung rightly contends that the tree of life is a common mother-symbol and that it may have been, in first instance, a fruit-bearing genealogical tree, hence a kind of tribal mother. He observed that numerous myths say that human beings came from trees and many of them tell how the hero was enclosed in the maternal tree. This is true to the Gikuyu myth, which relates the origin of the first man with the tree. The tree, the tribal mother, existed before Gikuyu, the father of the tribe. Thus, the tree is also one of the symbols of the Great Mother to whom we now turn.

a

CHAPTER FOURTEEN

Great Mother

The term great mother refers to the feminine quality which is predominant in women, but which is also found in a fully functioning male person. The archetypical motif of great mother is found in mythology and human history. She has both positive and negative aspects.

A. *The Myth and Reality of the Great Mother*

The Gikuyu myth includes two great women. The first one is Mumbi, the mother of the tribe and wife of Gikuyu, who had nine daughters and no sons. The name Mumbi means the creator and the molder.

The other woman hero is Wangu wa Makeri, who, unlike Mumbi, is both a historical and a mythical figure. Mythically, Wangu was a very successful warrior and a judge. But when she was at the peak of her reign, she became arrogant and danced naked. This act provoked men's anger and consequently she was dethroned. This ended the woman's reign in Gikuyu land.

However, I have interviewed several people in order to get historical facts about Wangu. According to James Makeri, the grandson of Wangu, the husband of Wangu, Makeri, was a very wealthy man. He had a big land, a large number of livestock, and men servants. He was also a man of great integrity. For these reasons he was respected by the Chief Justice Karuri wa Gakure. The former provided the latter with lodging on his way to Muranag's. Consequently they became great friends and, thus, Karuri requested Makeri whether he would like to be made a judge. Makeri refused and said that he would rather take care for his wealth, but recommended Wangu to Karuri. He informed Karuri that Wangu was a woman of great integrity and had leadership quality. Thus Wangu was made the leader. Eventually Wangu gained respect and became famous for her leadership. She had a strong army, which fought and won many battles. However, she only fought those who refused to comply with Karuri. The songs were composed about her victory. These songs were also urging those people who had not submitted to her to surrender to her and to the senior chief.

Muchiri Makeri, the stepson of Wangu argued thatWhat made Wangu famous was not the battles which she fought and won, but her work of reconciliation. She reconciled Karuri with many gikuyu families. On the one hand she persuaded people to support the chief justice and on the other, she persuaded Karuri not to fight those who were not rebels and those who had surrendered. In most cases, it was Wangu who ended the war by her diplomatic way of persuasion and reconciliation.

In addition, Wangu's home was a house of refuge. If someone committed a crime such as murder and was chased by people in order to be arrested and be killed, if he could run and reach Wangu's home before he was caught, that man was safe. Thus, Wangu saved many people who could have been killed. Another activity that made Wangu famous was the saving of innocent children who were being thrown to the hyena. According to the Gikuyu custom, if a woman gave birth to twins, their mouths were filled with grass and they were thrown to the bush to be devoured by the hyena. If a mother with a baby who was less than one year old died, the baby and the body of the deceased were taken to the bush to be consumed by the hyena. So Wangu wa Makeri ventured a new mission of saving these children. She instructed her soldiers how to save these children. The men had to wrestle with the hyena in order to save a baby. All the babies who were rescued were brought to Wangu's home where they were cared for by her. Muchiri said, "My main duty when I was a boy was to feed those babies with milk." Here we can see that Wangu was a forerunner of various organizations and institutions in Kenya, which are caring for destitute children.

Furthermore, Wangu was one of the first African leaders to realize that the first missionaries in Gikuyu land had something that was beneficial to the country. She studied McGregor of Weithaga Mission, her neighbor and found that he had something useful to offer - education. So she took some of the orphans to him. She urged her people, particularly those who were poor, to take their children to the missionary school. She also reconciled the missionaries with the chief justice. When she was reaching death, Wangu became a Christian and was baptized.

According to those who witnessed the dance, Wangu never danced naked. She had four pieces: the inner soft leather that covered her private part, an apron that covered her upper part, the skirt (Muthuru), and a long garment that covered her from neck to ankle known as riba, which is a long ceremonial dress like a long overcoat. It was this ceremonial dress, which Wangu removed in order that she could dance freely. Normally, one could not dance with a ceremonial dress.

Thus, Wangu was famous, not because of dancing naked, but owing to her hospitality, love, ministry of reconciliation, and transforming of Gikuyu tradition. She had the qualities of the ideal Great Mother.

B. *The Positivity of the Great Mother:*

The Great Mother as an archetype creates and repairs human relationships. She helps us to reach out, to join, to get in touch with, and be involved in concrete feelings, things, and people. She does not allow us to hang in the air, but pushes us right into the middle of events and things. Instead of being detached she involves us and urges us to be a part of happenings. She attracts us to the mode of being and relatedness.

In addition, the Great Mother connects us with our tradition. It is this essence that draws us to our mother-land so that we may be connected with our roots. It magnetizes us by in-going rather than out-going and then leads us to the dark womb in order that we may be reborn. By regestating us, the Great Mother generates new intuitions, fantasies, images, and drives. When this precious work is taking place, the images of water, home, cooking pot, cave, ark, coffin, and mountain appear in our dreams and fantasies.

And as we have seen in the myth of the Gikuyu female chief, the archetype of the Great Mother allows us to be mararanja. The story that narrates that Wangu danced naked expresses this quality, which is inherent in human personality. This archetype allows us to be irrational, ecstatic, and no moralistic. Its dynamism pushes us outside of the self and sets us free from the tribal taboos. It was this dynamism that drove Wangu to a mission of saving the babies, which were thrown to the hyenas. Saving these innocent twins was against the social norm of the time. The same dynamism empowered great men like William Wilberforce and Abraham Lincoln in their war against slavery.

This quality of the Great Mother allows us to be emotionally involved, to take risks, and, thereby, enlarge our ego boundaries. It inspires us and fills us with vitality. It throws us to the forces, which are above and beyond our limitations.

The Great Mother is the source of life and nourishment. In her and through her, an individual is soothed, comforted, and cherished. Nyumba (the mother's house) in which she dwells is the theatre of riddles, stories, and jokes. In this dwelling, an individual is free to be what Urban T. Holmes termed as a receptive mode of human consciousness. This mode of consciousness as opposed to action mode, processes experience in spatial images, in concrete rather than abstract ways, in holistic or relational over analytical or differentiated modes, in nonlinear terms rather than linear, analogically and not digitally, and through intuitive thinking as opposed to rational thought.

C. Negativity of the Great Mother

When the Great Mother gets sick, she expresses qualities that are opposed to those of a healthy one. Instead of being a refuge for her children, she devours them when they come to her for rescue. She scatters her children. She becomes impatient and does not allow her children to be in dark womb for nine months. She forces them out before a successful rebirth. And thus, they fail to move from one developmental stage to another. Said differently, the sick Great Mother has no patience for being with her children for forty years in the wilderness. She kills them before they have reached the Promised Land.

In addition, the sick mother may feel insecure and thus overprotect her children and deprive them mararanja expression, which facilitates the expansion of ego boundaries and self transcendence. She makes their lives static, rigid, and boring.

In addition to the house of the sick Great Mother, is the theatre of gossip and agitation. It is this sickness that is expressed by a Gikuyu proverb, "Women have no upright words, but only crooked ones". By her crooked words, the sick mother leads her children from light to darkness, from patient and love to uncontrollable anger, from repairing of relationship to destruction of human relationship, from sobriety to drunkenness, from self identity to ego diffusion, and from sanity to insanity.

The healthy mother, as we have seen, has a quality of reconciliation, relatedness, rebirth, traditionality, dynamism, and vitality. She repairs broken relationship. She is more interested in friendship. She values relationship more than riches. She makes every effort to reconcile her children with the Great Father.

a

CHAPTER FIFTEEN

The Great Father

The term Great Father will refer to the male aspect of human nature, which is predominately in men, but also found in fully functioning woman. The archetypal motif of the Great Father is evident in myths, idioms, and proverbs. He has both negative and positive aspect.

Structure and emotionlessness, which are the attributes of the Great Father, were demonstrated and ritualized on the actual day of circumcision. As we have seen, even the girls were not supposed to show any fear or make any audible sign of emotion or even blink. During the summit of pain, she demonstrated fearlessness. She was expected to be highly structured. The male initiated was expected to show the same mannerism. All the initiates were challenged by the Great Father to be highly structured and to confront fear and pain with courage.

Since irua dominated an individual from birth to death, this quality of the Great Father rained from childhood to death. I have always been astonished at this quality in one of my sisters. Mary cared for me when I was a baby and a little boy. To my surprise, I have never seen her crying. Occasionally, when she was a little girl, my father would pinch her ear lobe and cause bleeding, but Mary never cried or even showed any emotion. She manifested the same bravely in defending me against any prey.. One day, when we were herding, a boy who was bigger than Mary wanted to attack us, but Mary aimed at his forehead with a club, hit the boy, and knocked him down. I was amused the following day when the father of the boy came to report to my mother (this time my father had gone to glory) that Mary injured his son.

The other day, at age of sixty-eight, I reminded Mary of this incident. She bragged, "Even today, I am not yet old, and I do not allow anybody to step on my toes." This quality of life is typical to boys and girls who are unconsciously dominated by the actual day of circumcision. Since the archetype of the Great Father is within the collective unconscious, its quality is not limited to those who are initiated. It is inherent in uninitiated women as well. It is, indeed, found in all human families.

A. His Dwelling Places

The Great Father dwells in thingira (a traditional father's house). In thingira, one is challenged to be assertive and intentional. Here, mararanja dances are halted. The favorite proverb of the Great Father is, "Thiga has been circumcised, no more mararanja. " Meaning, since he is already circumcised, there is no more irrationality. This calls for economy of time and words. It also challenges and individual to be economically minded and precise.

While the Great Mother prefers stories, analogies, and metaphors, the Great Father favors a clear and logical language. The Great Mother entices us to be subjective. The Great Father urges us to be objective.

He enjoys sitting in parliament and in congress where he makes laws by which he governs and guides his children, in law courts where he judges and imprisons those who break the law, and in prison where he rehabilitates those whom he has imprisoned. Since the qualities of the great father are in both male and female, I do not, therefore, imply that the above institutions are or should be dominated by males. However, it is my argument that it is the qualities of the Great Father which are dominant in these institutions. To illustrates: During the staff institute of ATIEA, which I have already mentioned, I was in a team, which had to visit Arusha International Conference Center. After reaching this gigantic building, we were led to an office where we had to get someone who could take us around. Unfortunately, there was no one in the office. Consequently we waited for several minutes. In the meantime, we were attracted by a chart handing on the wall, which included the pictures of all the government ministers. For those of us who were not Tanzanian, it took us as a surprise to note that the official title of the ministers is Ndugu (Brother). Interestingly, there were pictures of two women ministers whose titles were Ndugu. These were Ndugu Jullie C. Manning, Wasiri wa Sheria (Brother Jullie C. Mnanning, the Minister of Law, and Ndugu Tabitha Siwale, Waziri wa Elimu ya Taifa (Brother Tabith Siwale, Minister for National Education. The use of the title Ndugu for a woman minister appeared to us as a contradiction in terms. However, our Tanzania friends informed us that the word Ndugu in this context meant a comrade. This was not convincing since the word Dada (Sister) could also convey the same meaning. Symbolically, I believe, the title Ndugu refers to the substance of the Great Father who makes laws and implement them in the government administration.

B. *The Substance of the Great Father*

Wisdom is another property of the Great Father. Interestingly, the Gikuyu ascribe all wise expressions, idioms, and proverbs to Gikuyu, the father of the tribe. For this reason, whenever a Gikuyu is using a proverb, he must credit the father of the tribe; it goes this way, "Gikuyu said, 'The day is for working, the night is for resting.'" It is as though the first father coined all the proverbs that guided the tribe in their daily living. The Great Father possesses the logos, which is the subtle fire emanating the whole universe. This logos is characterized by fire or light. This light illumines and guides the human family.

Initiative, assertiveness, creativity, and objectivity are other traits of the Great Father. He challenges us to venture into new projects, to declare our standpoint, and to be ourselves. He admonishes us not to waste time with petty things. He challenges us to be and to allow others to be…. In this regard, the Gikuyu justify their individuality with a proverb, "One does not structure his family as that of his age mate." This meant that even though the age set underwent the same school, every person was an individual. For that reason, the Gikuyu discouraged over-identification. A person who aped another person was rebuked. If for instance, Mwangi noticed that Njoroge was over-identifying himself with Kamau, Mwangi would shout, "Kamau identification!" (Kamau Kanyi), meaning, you are not yourself but a false Kamau. Thus the Great Father urges us to be ourselves.

In his negative expression, the Great Father may ignore the collective responsibility and concentrate on his own personal interest. For instance, the Great Father in the parliament may use his influential position as a means of appropriating wealth and oppressing the community that has voted for him. He may become corrupt and ignore the law. He may defend the "haves" and deny justice to the "have-nots."

The Great Father may become power-thirsty and unreachable to his children. In this negativity, he becomes as a lion or an elephant that crushes to death those who may be the future leaders. He may become autocratic and have no interest in consensus of opinion. This destructive behavior creates a personality that is more interested in power than progress.

The sick Great Father may be imbued with aggression and wreck his family. In this case, he became moody and always attacking children, depriving them of freedom of expression and being, which are necessary for personality development. He may also order his children to attack other people and spend government revenue with unnecessary wars. In so doing he provokes other nations to war. This may result to global recession. In this case, the Great Father ignores other aspect to life so as to equip his hunting dog.

When he gets sick, the Great Father may ignore his own responsibilities and take the responsibility of others. To use a Gikuyu proverbs, "He roofs other people's huts while his own hut is leaking," "He disregards his own log while he tries to take the speck from his neighbor's eye," "He attributes all the goodness and strength in the community to himself while projecting his garbage to others," "Instead of repenting his own sin he tries to convince the whole world that all evil resides in those around him."

Another negative aspect of the Great Father is *absent farness*. By absent farness I refer to a permanent removal of the father's house from the homestead, and building it in a far country. In this case, the father is permanently away from the family. He leaves his family in the countryside and goes to the town to earn a living. This mode of life is becoming the order of the day in Kenya. The degree of absent farness varies. Some husbands who live away from their families may visit their home once a month or once a year to take some money, and of course to manufacture more children to whom they will never give day-to-day guidance and emotional support. Others stay in their working place with concubines or prostitutes and, therefore, squander all their money. They may stay for years without visiting their families. The extremist category is that of the husbands who have totally deserted their families with no hope of being reunited again. The last category is that of the families who do not know what it is to have a father. The mother has never been married, yet she has a family of which she is the head and a potential provider. Needless to say, the case of absentee fathers is crucial in East Africa. It has been estimated that 60 percent of the husbands do not stay with their families. This is a new phenomenon, since traditionally the father's dwelling was located within the homestead. Here he guided, protected, and sustained the family. His sons and daughters had someone to imitate. They had a father who could enforce discipline. At present the majority of the mothers are left alone with their children. In most cases, they are both the bread winners and the heads of families. In all cases of absentee fathers, the mother is in charge of the day to day running of the family. She is the head of the family. This issue of the absenteeism of fathers is indeed ushering in a new era in African society. We are possibly in a transitional period, moving from a patriarchal society to a matriarchal society. This society will have a real problem with the authority figures. It will have no respect for the rule of the law, which is the product of the Great Father. Possibly, this society will find it easier to unite behind a system rather than a person.

The sick Great Father may be unforgiving and legalistic, expecting his children not only to obey every code of law but also may expect them to live in accordance with his whims. He may also be too involved and, therefore, pay little attention to trivial matters. He may be hunting for gossip and rumor and use them as criteria for judging and punishing his children. This type of involvement is what we term *destructive nearness*. When the Great Father has this type of nearness, he deprives his children of freedom of expression and of being, which is vital for their ego development. He robs them of wisdom, which is acquired through trial and error.

In conclusion, the positive qualities of the Great Father include structure, assertiveness, intentionality, judgment, rehabilitation, wisdom, initiative, and creativity. His negative characteristics are comprised of aggressiveness, absent farness, destructive nearness, irresponsibility, legalism and, authoritarianism.

a

CHAPTER SIXTEEN

Summary

It is evident that human personality needs to balance between individuality and communality. One should be himself in order that he may make his unique contribution to society. He should be communal so that he may draw from and become a part of the community.

Furthermore, it is obvious that we are fundamentally sexual beings. Sexuality, being vital spiritual energy, generates a loving, warm. and cordial feeling toward one another. For this reason, sex should never be abused nor regarded as a "forbidden fruit." Thus, we need to develop a more positive theology and psychology of human sexuality.

In addition, we have found that we cannot do away with the division of labor since it helps an individual to know his/her role in the community. However, with the emergence of urbanization, modernization, and professionalism, the division of labor needs to be redefined so that no one is overworked or exploited.

Similarly, it has become clear that we have antistructured and structured spheres. The antistructured realm of our personality is irrational and chaotic. Yet, it is vital since a deeper interpersonal relationship is attained only when the antistructure is reached and appreciated. On the other hand, the structured sphere is orderly, rational, and intentional. We have argued that we need to balance between the structured self and the unstructured self. We should know where and when to be either structured or antistructured.

We have also noted that lostness is a part and parcel of the rite of passage. During the "passages" we may undergo a period of confusion, conflict, disorientation, and precariousness.

The lostness may be either communal or individual. It may have a positive or negative result. We have argued that during the situation, an individual needs to be guided and illumined rather than being excommunicated or ostracized.

Moreover, we have seen that pain is a reality. It is evident in the life and teaching of Christ. Pain can either deter or facilitate personality growth. It may lead to faithlessness, inferiority feelings, ego diffusion, self absorption, stagnation, and despair, or instill faith, hope, love integrity, insight, and wisdom. In addition, we have dealt with the three great archetypal motifs of the psyche: the Tree of God, the Great Mother, and the Great Father. We have asserted that here is the communal tree and the individual tree. The Tree of God connects us with and makes us conscious of our primordial time, the totality of our ontology, and the complexity and ambiguity of our environment. The myths, reality, positivity and negativity of the Great Mother and the Great Father have been discussed.

In counseling, we must first discover our archetypal motifs and find out how we relate to them. As an analyst, we must psychoanalyze ourselves in order that we may be able to psychoanalyze others. We should, for instance, endeavor to discover the phenomena, the objects, persons, and personality types that evoke the archetypes of the Tree of God, the Great Mother, and the Great Father. After discovering our particular archetypes, we should try to discover those of our clients and find out how they relate to them. We may find that the person who has a sick religion may fear to face the Tree of God, which, to a large extent, is symbolized by the holy shrines and religious specialists. A woman who has a sick Great Father may have a problem with or exploit males. A Gikuyu woman who has this problem likes to use a sweeping statement, "Never trust men, for they are animals." Similarly, a man who has a problem with the inner Great Mother will have problems with females. He, too, likes to use a sweeping statement, "Never show a woman your wisdom tooth." Meaning never smile to or laugh with a woman. He may treat his wife and other women as sexual objects. In all cases, the counselor should help these individuals to face and learn to relate to the Tree of God, the Great Mother, and the Great Father since sanctification of life, self-identity, and integrity depend on how we relate to these great archetypal motifs of the psyche. The three are the filters through which we receive the heavenly and earthly grace, which facilitates the movement from glory to glory. The more we allow the water of life to filter through them, the more we grow to wholeness. This growth leads to joy, love, faith, insight, and wisdom.

a

ENDNOTES

CHAPTER TWO

1. Jomo Kenyatta,. *Facing Mount Kenya* (London: Secker and Warburg, 1971).

G. Parrinder, *West African Psychology* (London: Lutterworth, 1976).

L. S. B. Leakey, *The Southern Kikuyu Before 1903*. (New York: Academic Press, 1977).

CHAPTER THREE

1. Jomo Kenyatta gives a detailed description of ngwiko in his *Facing Mount Kenya,* 155-162.

2. John S. Mbiti, *African Religions and Philosophy* (location?: Publisher?, year?), 113.

3. Leakey, *The Southern Kikuyu* (locaton?: Publisher?, year), 155.

4. Jesse Mugambi and Nicodemus Kirima, *The African Religious Heritage* (Nairobi: Oxford University Press, 1976), 20.

5. Ibid., 20.

6. Ibid., 20.

[7]Mugo Gatheru, *The Child of Two Worlds* (location?: Publisher?, year?), 21.

[8]Permenas Gathendu Mockerie, *African Speaks for his People* (London: Leonard and Virginia, 1934), 36.

CHAPTER FOUR

1. Raymond J Corsin, *Current Personality Theories* (Illinois: F. E Peacok, 1977), 15.

2. *?*

3. See Sigmud Freud. *The Sexual Enlightenment of Children* (Toronto: Macmillan, 1969).

4. ?

5. Erik H Erikson, *Childhood and Society* (New York: Fordham University Press, year??), 259

6. Perter L. Berger and Thomas Luckman. *Social Construction of Reality.* (New York: Double Day, 1966) p.1

CHAPTER FIVE

By word motif, I mean important, recurrent salient themes in an individual's pilgrimage. These themes are also inherent in the community's life cycle.

Rudolf Bultmann, *Jesus and the World* (London: Fantana, 1962), 11.

Martin Debelius, *Jesus* (London: publisher?, 1963), 8.

William Barclay, *The First Three Gospels* (London: Bloombury, 1966), 14.

Donald Baillie, *The Mediator* (London: Fantana, 1934), 184.

The nativity stories in Matthew 2:14 and Luke 2:39 should not be considered as pure history. As Raymond E. Brown says, "They agree in so few details that we may say with certainty that they cannot both be historical in toto. (Brown, *The Virginal Conception and Bodily Resurrection of Jesus*

(New York: Paulist, 1973), 54.)

CHAPTER FIVE

By word motif, I mean important, recurrent salient themes in an individual's pilgrimage. These themes are also inherent in the community's life cycle.

Rudolf Bultmann, *Jesus and the World* (London: Fantana, 1962), 11.

Martin Debelius, *Jesus* (London: publisher??, 1963), 8.

William Barclay, *The First Three Gospels* (London: Bloombury, 1966), 14.

Donald Baillie, *The Mediator* (London: Fantana, 1934), 184.

The nativity stories in Matthew 2:14 and Luke 2:39 should not be considered as a pure history. As Raymond E. Brown says, "They agree in so few details that we may say with certainty that they cannot both be historical in toto. (Brown, *The Virginal Conception and Bodily Resurrection of Jesus* (New York: Paulist, 1973), 54.)

CHAPTER SEVEN

See the Commission's Report: Author??, *Sex and Morality* (Philadelphia: Fortress, 1966), 64.

Kosnik, et al., *Human Sexuality* (New York: Paulist Press, 1977), 1.

Mukami Ireri, "Can Women Escape Being Bought?" *Viva*, March, 1982, p#?.

Hans Kung, *On Being a Christian* (New York: Doubleday, 1976), 261.

Kosnik, et al., *Human Sexuality* (New York: Paulist Press, 1977), 8.

Sigmund Freud, *The Sexual Enlightenment of Children* (Toronto: Collier Book, 1969), 19.

Ibid., p.19

Freud employs the word Trieb for instinct. Trieb is more related to the word "drive." He used the word to refer to an impetus and impelling force within the mind, which has effects on both psychic equilibrium and development.

Erwin J. Haeberie, *The Sex Atlas* (New York: The Seabury, 1978), 146.

CHAPTER EIGHT

Two most useful books in type-matching are Bates and Kiersey, *Please Understand Me* (Del Mar, CA: Prometheus Nemisis Books, 1978) and

Kroeger and Thuesen, *Type Talk* (New York: Dell Publishing, 1988).

CHAPTER TEN

Booty and Thomas, *The Spirit of Anglicanism* (Connecticut: Morehouse-Barlow, 1979), 8

2. Otto Rank, *Beyond Psychology* (New York: Dover Pub., 1958), 124

CHAPTER ELEVEN

1. S.K. Lutahoire, *The Human Life Cycle Among the Bantu*

(Arusha: Makumira Publication, 1974), 56

2 ibid., 56

a

Appendix

As it has been noted, the initiation rites determined the name of the year, and the greatest event of the year established the name of the age group. For instance, the age group which was initiated when the first airplane appeared (1927) was called airplane (Ndege). If there appeared locust that devastated the crops and caused great famine (1889) both the age group and the year were named locust. And thus, the initiation chronicled the history of the people.

The following is the list of the Gikuyu age groups (marika ma Agikuyu)

a

MARIKA	IRUA	BORN MALE	BORN FEMALE
KAMAU	1841	1824	1827
KARANJA	1842	1825	1828
NJUGUNA	1843	1826	1829
NDUATI	1944	1827	1830
KINUTHIA	1945	1828	1831
KIMANI	1946	1829	1832
GUTHURU	1847	1830	1833
KINYANJUI	1848	1831	1834
NG'ANG'A	1849	1832	1835
NJOROGE YAGIKONDE	1850	1833	1836
NJOROGE YA MUNYONGORO	1851	1834	1837
GATHITA	1852	1835	1838
WAMUHIA, KINUTHIA	1853	1836	1839
WANYENI	1854	1837	1840
THINGITHA	1855	1838	1841
GITAU	1856	1839	1842
NJIHIA	1857	1840	1843
WAINAINA	1858	1841	1844
KANG'ETHE	1859	1842	1845
CHOMBA	1860	1843	1846
MUNGAI	1861	1844	1847
MWAURA	1862	1845	1848
MAIRANG'A	1863	1846	1849
WARAGA	1864	1847	1850
MNGUOCHIA, MANGUCHIA	1865	1848	1851
MBUGUA	1867	1850	1853

KIRURA	1868	1851	1854
GITINDIKO	1869	1852	1855
MUTUNG'U	1870	1853	1856
MUIRURI	1871	1854	1857
KIAMBUTHIA	1872	1855	1858
NGUGI	1873	1856	1859
MANG'URIU	1874	1857	1860
KUHANG'IA	1875	1858	1861
KINUBU	1876	1859	1862
HUCHI	1877	1860	1863
NGUNGA	1878	1861	1864
NJAURA, NJAURE	1879	1862	1865
WANJOIKE	1880	1863	1866
BORO GATHAMIA	1881	1864	1867
KINITI	1882	1865	1868
RUHONGE	1883	1866	1869
KIANJANE	1884	1867	1870
NGARUMA	1885	1868	1871
KIROBU, MUGURU	1886	1869	1872
MBURU,NGOMA YA MURU	1887	1870	1873
UHERE	1888	1871	1874
NGIGI	1889	1872	1875
MURERA	1890	1873	1876
MUTUNGU	1891	1874	1877
UNUBI,RUHARO	1892	1885	1878
KAGICHA	1893	1876	1879
KIBIRI	1894	1877	1880
NJAGATHI	1995	1878	1881

MING'OTE, MWING'TE	1896	1879	1882
NDUTU, NUTHI	1897	1880	1883
KIENJEKU	1898	1881	1884
MUTHURA, DIMU YA CHUMA	1899	1882	1885
NG'RAGU YA RURAYA	1900	1883	1886
GATEGO, HITI	1901	1884	1887
KAMANDE, GATITI, KING'ORA	1902	1885	1888
KIBANGO, NDONGORO	1903	1886	1889
NJEGE, GIKURA	1904	1887	1890
KANYUTU, NYUTU	1905	1888	1891
NYARIGI, WARIGI	1906	1889	1892
KANG'ETI	1907	1890	1893
MATIBA, KABAU,GITONGE	1908	1891	1994
THIGINGI	1909	1892	1995
MAKIO	1910	1893	1896
NGIMBI, NGARAGU YA GATHEA	1911	1894	1897
MANDE, MWENDE, NJARAMBA	1912	1895	1898
KIHIU MWIRI	1913	1896	1899
RUMEMO	1914	1897	1900
NGAIKIA	1915	1898	1901

NGOMERA (NGUIKA) NGOIGE	1916	1899	1902
NJANE, NJANJO, KIGENGI	1883	1866	1869
GITHONGO, NDARAMA	1917	1900	1903
NG'ARAGU YA KIMOTHO	1918	1901	1904
KAHURI, KABIARU	1919	1902	1905
KIBANDE, IGUTA	1920	1903	1906
MUNANDA	1921	1904	1907
MUNETI	1922	1905	1908
CHIRINGI	1923	1906	1909
GITHIGU	1924	1907	1910
MUNAI	1925	1908	1911
KIANDUMA	1926	1909	1912
NDEGE, NDEGE YA MBERE	1927	1910	1913
GITHINGITHIA	1928	1911	1914
NGIGI,NDEREGE	1929	1912	1915
MAMBOLEO, KARARA	1930	1913	1916
MAROBO, KANYUI	1931	1914	1917
NJANE KANINI	1931	1915	1918
NJENDURA	1932	1916	1919
NDURURU, NGARAGU	1933	1917	1920
YA KARUGIA MITHURU	1934	1918	1921
TAURU	1935	1919	1922

KENYA MBATHI,KIGOTO	1936	1920	1923
KARABA, NJABANI,MBORO	1937	1921	1924
THUKIA MATAHA, GICHURI	1938	1922	1925
MUCHITHI WA MBIA	1940	1923	1926
MUTHUU	1941	1924	1927
NGARAGU YA MIANGA	1942	1925	1928
BAMETI	1943	1926	1929
MWOMBOKO	1944	1927	1930
GIGINA FANGI	1945	1928	1931
NJATA	1946	1929	1932
NGOMA KIBIRITI	1947	1930	1933
HARAKA	1948	1931	1934
KAYU	1949	2932	1935
MUHEHENJEKO	1950	1933	1936
THUTU	1951	1934	1937
WARURUNGANA	1952	1935	1938
KOMERERA	1953	1936	1939
GOTORA	1954	1937	1940
THERENDA	1955	1938	1941
CENI	1956	1939	1942
RUTHARIO	1957	1940	1943
MUBUTITI NGEITHIA THAYU	1958	1941	1944
NGEITHIA NDIMURUU	1959	1942	1945

a

www.ingramcontent.com/pod-product-compliance
Lightning Source LLC
Chambersburg PA
CBHW032051020426
42335CB00011B/287